Preface

This is a lay person's handbook for renewing the Catholic church. Your renewal of the church can begin immediately. It needs no one's approval. It depends totally on you and your fellow Catholics. It is certainly not beyond your abilities. All it takes is courage–courage to stand up to the hierarchy, the current leadership of our church, courage not to be satisfied with their lies, their underhanded practices, and their centuries-long arrogance. This reform will be effective beyond your wildest hopes, because it copies a great model, the one depicted in the New Testament, the one begun by Jesus.

There is one difference between *Talking Treason in Church* and anything else written by Catholics on the current state of the church. Catholics today have written brilliant analyses of what's wrong with the church, but when they come to the end of their book or their article–where you would expect to see proposed solutions–what you read is all wishful thinking: the church *should* listen more to the lay people, the hierarchy *has to be* more open to structural change.

Or their book or article demands intensive lobbying of the hierarchy by the laity, thousands and thousands of hours spent by lay people in forming groups, getting up petitions, trying by every possible means of persuasion and political pressure to move the hierarchy from their position of intransigence and inattention.

It's all pie in the sky! Why should the laity make super-human efforts while nothing can be required of the hierarchy?

We're dealing with the same narrow, self-interested, ignorant, arrogant, hard-nosed hierarchy that flouted, persecuted, and killed every reformer it could lay its hands on five centuries ago. Some hierarchs at least would do the same today if the judgment of the entire world were not against them. They are creatures of power in a structure of power that deserves to be uprooted. And thanks basically to the progress of learning, that project is now doable.

At the same time, it is important to point out that what we are taking aim at is not personalities. It is a ruling idea, the idea of hierarchy. It comprises everything that is wrong with the Catholic church: papacy, papal court, subordination of bishops, priestly rule, and utter contempt for the laity. We are not opposed to the many good priests and bishops who are part of the Catholic church and who feel the burden of hierarchy in some ways more than the laity do. In fact these priests and bishops are our natural allies.

The one difference between this book and everything preceding it is that it presents a practical solution, a way in which lay people can begin at once to renew the Catholic church. This book demonstrates through an examination of Christian origins that the church began with the laity and that the controlling power of the church remains in our hands, if we have but the sense to use it.

Talking Treason in Church was prompted by several insights.

First, Jesus Christ was a lay person, not a priest, and the movement of reform that he began in Judaism was a lay movement. The chief priests, the hierarchy of his time, considered him a threat and had him put to death by the Romans.

Second, neither the Catholic priesthood nor the Catholic hierarchy existed during the first century of our era. There is no scriptural nor historical basis for either one at that time. In fact, the Mass, the center of Catholic sacramental life was, during the first century, celebrated by lay people and, notably in the earliest days of the church, by women in their own homes.

Third, the hierarchical priesthood, when it began to emerge during the second through the fourth centuries, was strongly influenced by the model of the Roman imperial administration. It also drew on examples of priesthoods throughout the ancient world including that of Israel. It was a movement toward the kind of religious specialization that was familiar in the ancient world. But it owed nothing to the teaching of Jesus Christ.

Fourth, the foundation myth of the Roman Catholic church as propounded by the hierarchy makes St. Peter the first bishop of Rome. That myth is made up of so many historical fallacies that any member of the hierarchy with even a smattering of historical education should be embarrassed to cite it. But by some of the

Talking Treason in Church

The Lay Person's Guide
To Renewing the Catholic Church

By Joseph P. Marren, M.A.

iUniverse - Bloomington, IN

Talking Treason in Church
(The Lay Person's Guide to Renewing the Catholic Church)

iUniverse books may be ordered through booksellers or by contacting:

iUniverse
1663 Liberty Drive
Bloomington, IN 47403
www.iuniverse.com
1-800-Authors (1-800-288-4677)

Because of the dynamic nature of the Internet, any Web addresses or links contained in this book may have changed since publication and may no longer be valid.

ISBN: 978-1-4401-9517-4 (sc)
ISBN: 978-1-4401-9518-1 (ebk)

Printed in the United States of America

iUniverse rev. date: 12/16/2009

*For my children and grandchildren
and for the Catholic Church*

*If you wish to see change in the world,
you must be the change you wish to see.
—Mohandas Gandhi*

Table of Contents

hierarchy this myth is used knowingly as a political construct to support their will to power. These members of the hierarchy are conscious liars and deserve no place in the Catholic church.

Fifth, the Catholic hierarchy, the pope and the bishops, down through the centuries have been sometimes more and sometimes considerably less successful at asserting their exclusive right to rule the church. In fact, there are enough instances in the early church of the popular election of bishops to provide a controlling precedent for our time.

Sixth, today, the Catholic laity are totally excluded by the hierarchy from choosing their religious leaders or having any discourse whatsoever with the leadership of the church. The effect has been to erect a wall of separation between the hierarchy and the laity. This is a serious sin on the part of the bishops, a sin against the Holy Spirit who dwells in lay people at least as much as in the hierarchy. It is called schism. It has created a paralysis in the church which gives the hierarchy–and the rest of us by extension–the appearance of being brain-dead.

The hierarchy have laid themselves open to a number of criticisms straight out of the New Testament. The chief one we should instance now is: "You have nullified the word of God for the sake of your tradition. Hypocrites, well did Isaiah prophesy about you when he said:

> "'This people honors me with their lips, but
> their hearts are far from me; in vain do they
> worship me, teaching human precepts as
> doctrines.'"

(Mt 15: 6-9)

That is precisely what the Catholic hierarchy are guilty of. When asked to justify their hierarchical rule, they point to authorities that they themselves have trumped up, human traditions tricked out as divine doctrines. It won't wash. For as Jesus says in discussing marriage and divorce, "From the beginning, it was not so." (Mt 19:8)

The sum of all these charges is that the current leadership of the Catholic Church, the hierarchy, are the wolves in sheep's clothing, the hirelings who care nothing for the sheep, that Jesus Christ foretold in the gospels. They are imposters. Because they have not submitted themselves to a vote of the lay people before assuming office, their ordinations are invalid. The vast church of lay Catholics throughout the world cannot and does not depend upon them; they depend upon us for their continued support. Thus there is really no question of talking treason against them. We have rather the duty under God to oust them from office as soon as possible. But we should recognize what we are up against.

The mindset of the Official Catholic Church is still that of a totalitarian government. It rules through threats and intimidation. If threats do not work, it adopts an attitude of passive aggression. It simply refuses to cooperate. It hides its doings under a cloak of secrecy, refuses to respond, refuses to communicate. But it cannot continue this pose without the support of masses of lay people. And the fact is that the laity in the United States have been leaving the church in droves. The children of strong Catholic families simply have not continued the practice of the faith in which they were raised. They don't consider the (Official Catholic) Church relevant to their lives. And they are right. Anecdotal evidence suggests that the same situation exists throughout the Western world. So the Official Catholic Church governing system is doomed in any case, even without our efforts, under the impulse, I believe, of the Holy Spirit.

What do we Catholic lay people do about this situation? That is the question this book tries to answer. The answer in brief is, We go back to basics. With the lessons of 2000 years of history to guide us, we go back to the "structure" of the early church. We retake control of the church, which is ourselves, from a fundamentally discredited and fraudulent governing class–and we do it, not through passive aggression, not through exhausting and pointless agitation, but through actively reviving the practices of the early church in our own parishes and among ourselves. We go back to being led by the Holy Spirit, back to recognizing people's charisms, not shoehorning them into offices for which they may not be well suited. As Hans Küng points out, charisms *serve* the community of the church; offices *dominate over* it.[1]

The hierarchy have poured concrete over the fertile fields of the church, but after centuries the concrete is old and broken,

---

[1]   *The Catholic Church: A Short History*, Hans Küng, tr. John Bowden, Modern Library, NY, 2001, p. 8.

and flowers of faith are springing up everywhere. Our job is to clear the fields, cart away the concrete, and return the land to productive life. The Lord has supplied us with the tools. Now it's up to us.

When you reach the end, or even the middle, of this book, you will see why we're on the right track in taking Jesus' example for renewing the Catholic church. The reform proposed here is a lay person's reform like the reform that Jesus started. It supplies the answers to some of the most long-felt and troubling questions asked by the laity over the last several decades.

The priest shortage decried by laity and clergy alike has us focusing on the wrong goal. There is no priest shortage. In fact, we have too many priests. What we don't have enough of is people to celebrate Mass. But then, actually, we do have enough people. They simply don't know that it is part of their birthright as Catholics to have the Mass when and where they want it.

Women's ordination asks the question, Why can't we have women priests? It's the wrong question. Why not ask why women can't be leaders in the church? The answer to both questions is, Clearly women can be leaders in the church, and women can say Mass. Priesthood has nothing to do with it.

For years we have prayed for vocations. Well, our prayers have all been answered long since. We simply have to be alive to the promptings of the Holy Spirit. Just as he promised, Jesus has not left us orphans.

Catholics for years have questioned clerical celibacy. Certainly this requirement does not go back to the apostles who, except for St. Paul, were very likely all married. This requirement has kept many men from the priesthood. Is there any way to do away with it? Yes. Again we're asking the wrong question. It seems evident that the hierarchy laid this heavy burden upon their subjects in the middle ages so that no church property would be left to priests' heirs. The problem is the hierarchy and their concern over losing property. As for married men saying Mass, that is not a problem.

One troubling last question remains for those of us who study the signs of the times. Why is it that the Holy Spirit has chosen *this* time to launch the fundamental renewal of the Catholic church? What demands loom ahead of us for which a renewed, autonomous, and greatly decentralized church must be prepared?

I don't want to speculate very much on this subject. I would point out, however, that the present Catholic church government is a vast network, all of whose initiatives, commands, and disciplines come from Rome. Picture a worldwide cataclysm in which the global web of almost instantaneous communications and easy travel are disrupted for a long period, and local churches are forced to continue on their own. The present hierarchy are ill equipped mentally or spiritually for that eventuality.

The Lay Catholic Renewal movement will be equal to such a challenge. May it never come!

A "Loyal Opposition" in the Catholic Church?

Is there room in the Catholic church for a Loyal Opposition?

Loyal in the sense that it reveres the church of the past and the present for all of its good works and its striving for holiness in the following of Jesus Christ.

Loyal in its desire to support the priests and sisters whose numbers are declining, who are being neglected in their old age.

But Opposition that rejects the way in which leadership is currently selected and exercised in the Catholic church.

Opposition to the current structure of the church because it is supported upon a rickety framework of lies and half-truths that only cloud the minds of the unwary, secure power to the present leadership, and keep the great mass of the church in a state of ignorance and graceless subserviency.

The church is not simply a divine institution. It is an amalgam, both divine and human. This is a key insight. Jesus Christ founded the church, but our human response to that foundation, the ways in which we Catholics have chosen to worship God, the structures and practices we have created—almost all that we now call the Catholic religion—is of human manufacture. Even Baptism was invented by John the Baptist, or at least adapted by him from Jewish tradition. The only practice left us by Jesus Christ is the Eucharist.

And it seems obvious that the Catholic church, in the sense of the religious structure we have put in place, is in dire need, not of reform—because that would leave the same human constitution in place—but of a revolution! A revolution like that produced by Jesus Christ in the Jewish "church." A revolution like the American Revolution, in which Americans accepted the English tradition in everything but the monarchy and out of that tradition produced a nation governed by its own people.

We need a thoroughgoing revolution to free the energies of Catholics to make the best of their tradition and to downgrade or eliminate values that are purely organizational and anti-Christian.

1

What are the grounds for this revolution? The signs are easy to see.

- Take the Mass, for example. The Mass is the birthright of every Catholic Christian. It is the one thing that the Lord asked us to do in his memory. Yet because of the current organizational values in the Catholic church, the Mass, with its ability to focus and renew the Catholic Christian community, is denied to hundreds of thousands, if not millions, of Catholics every week because there is no priest available.

  This is wrong. It may be Catholic tradition now, but it was not so in the beginning. The New Testament knows nothing of a Catholic priesthood such as we have at present—a kind of trade union without which no Eucharist can be held. It is time for this tradition to be uprooted.

  As a matter of cold, hard fact, the earliest Masses, as we know from St. Paul's letters, were conducted in people's homes, in house churches by ordinary people. Since many of the earliest Christians were, in fact, Gentiles who had converted to the Jewish faith and who then came to believe that Jesus was the Messiah, many of the leaders of these house churches in Gentile communities were women. It was far easier for women to become Jews than for men, since women didn't have to be circumcised. And since Mass was celebrated by the leaders of the house churches, it is inevitable that women who were not priests in our sense celebrated some of the first Masses.[2]

---

[2] In light of the subsequent patriarchal history of the Catholic church, it is sobering to recall that Jesus Christ broke with the social and religious conventions of his time by speaking on equal terms with women (John: 4: 4-42, the Samaritan woman at the well; esp. v. 27), by having women friends (Martha and Mary; Luke 10:38ff; John 11:1-44), and by permitting women to travel with him in his entourage (Luke 8:1-3).

St. Paul continued that theme in his gospel. He gives it the clearest expression in his Letter to the Galatians. For you who have put on Christ, i.e., become members of the church, he says "there is no Jew nor Greek, there is no slave nor free person, there is no man nor woman, for all of you are one in the Messiah, Jesus" (Gal 3:28).

Paul underscored the equality of men and women in the church by recognizing a great number of women as fellow workers [Prisca and Aquila, Rom. 16:3], missionary apostles [Andronicus and Junia, Rom. 16:7], and ministers [Phoebe, Rom. 16:1]. Prisca and Aquila and Andronicus and Junia

Today, it is taken for granted that the Catholic multitudes in the rural areas of Latin America and other parts of the world may celebrate Scripture services and even bring new Catholics into the church through Baptism. The one thing they may not do is precisely what Jesus asked them to do, remember him in the Eucharist. This is nonsense!

• Take another example, the papacy. Looked at coldly and objectively, the papacy is the longest surviving totalitarian government in the world today. It is modeled exactly on the Roman Empire of the second, third, and fourth centuries, which divided imperial administrative districts into dioceses and archdioceses. In time the empire disappeared as an organic unity, but the church modeled on it did not. If the Italians had not taken from the pope the Papal States in 1860 and the City of Rome in 1870, the pope would still be a temporal autocrat and far less of a spiritual leader than he is today.

The papacy's adherents would have you believe that Jesus instituted that office when he said to Peter, "Thou art Peter (a rock), and upon this rock I will build my church" and when he gave him the keys to the kingdom of heaven and the power of binding and loosing (Matt. 16:18-19). But these arguments are self-serving in the mouth of a hierarchical church. They are made by the papacy and its promoters to consolidate power over their fellow Catholics in the hands of the hierarchy. Otherwise they are made out of ignorance and because, "That's the way it's always been." In other words by appeal to an unexamined "tradition."

This tradition, too, deserves to be rooted up, because, whatever else St. Peter may have been, he was not the first bishop of Rome, he was not the first leader of the Roman Christian community, and in fact he died before the notion of bishop (Greek: *episkopos*) as monarchical leader of the Christian community came into existence.

St. Paul, before coming to Rome for the first time, writes his longest and most carefully worded letter, to the Romans,

---

were, of course, married couples. But each is treated as an equal in the work of evangelization. Prisca is the woman in the first couple named, and Junia in the second couple.

probably about 55-56 CE.[3] Several facts are clear. There is
already a Christian community at Rome. It consists of both
Jews and former Gentiles. Peter is not then at Rome; otherwise, Paul, who had met and talked with him for some weeks
shortly after his own conversion, would have sent him greet-
ings in the letter. Thus Peter could not then have been that
community's sole leader. The community has leaders, but
Peter is not one of them. The leadership that exists is evidently
communal, a leadership of cooperation in the service of the
gospel.

The Acts of the Apostles depicts Paul's first visit to
Rome—as a prisoner. Acts does not finish Paul's story. We
are indebted to tradition for the knowledge that Paul was freed
from prison, left Rome, and later returned to meet his death
along with Peter, probably in the persecution of Nero in 64 CE.
Clement, writing for the church of Rome to the church of
Corinth probably about 96 CE, mentions the deaths of Peter
and Paul. He calls them the "good apostles" and "the greatest
and most righteous pillars of the church." But even though
Clement's purpose in his letter is to establish good order under
bishops (or "overseers," "administrators") and presbyters
("elders"), he does not call Peter or Paul by either of these
titles. The whole tenor of his letter makes it clear that the monarchical episcopate does not yet exist in Rome.

Ignatius of Antioch is the first and strongest proponent of
the bishop as sole ruler in the church. Shortly before his
martyrdom (ca. 107 CE), he writes seven letters to various
churches throughout the Mediterranean world, including Rome,
strongly advocating the monarchical episcopate. The very
urgency of his assertions, however, shows that that institution
does not yet exist in most of the churches of his time.

The earliest succession lists of bishops of Rome date from
160 CE (Hegesippus) and 180 CE (Irenaeus of Lyons). It is
about this time that the notion of one-man rule in the Roman
church begins to take hold. So about this time, shared leadership among prophets, teachers, and elders has probably given

---

[3] CE and BCE are used instead of A.D. and B.C. in deference to other
religions. CE stands for Common Era; BCE for Before the Common Era.

way to a minimally shared leadership by the single administrator, the bishop. The succession lists were therefore made up to trace into the past the line of succession back to the apostles. This activity retroactively made "bishops" of community leaders who were not in fact monarchical or, as we now say, hierarchical leaders in their own times.

In short, the pope's claim to monarchical leadership of the church is specious, since even St. Peter, from whom he claims to take his example, did not exercise such leadership in the Roman church. Peter must have had a place of honor in the Roman church as the most important apostle. Whatever leadership he had, however, was shared with St. Paul, if they were in Rome at the same moment, but certainly was shared with the leaders of the Roman church, who were there before him.

Once the political debris is cleared away from the texts recounting Jesus' giving to St. Peter the "power of the keys" and the "power of binding and loosing," the church will be able to concentrate on finding out what the true spiritual meaning of those texts is. It could well be that Jesus was illustrating the qualities that should enable the church as a whole to discern its true leaders. In this case, these passages would have nothing to do with priesthood, papacy, gender, or celibacy. They would have to do with faithfulness, spiritual insight, the ability to nourish the faith of others, and the ability to show where the Spirit of God is leading.

- Take another example. Why does the Roman Catholic church have a priesthood? Despite what the present leadership of the church asserts in this matter, Jesus Christ was not a priest. He could not be a priest. He was of the house and family of David, which was not a priestly house. True, the author of the Letter to the Hebrews does call Jesus a priest, in fact "our great High Priest." But that is a metaphor to point out to the author's Jewish contemporaries the superiority of Jesus' redemptive death and true atonement for the sins of the world in comparison to the actions of the Jewish High Priest, who entered the Holy of Holies in the Temple once a year, and every year, repeatedly, to attempt to atone for the sins of the people.[4]

The Jewish priesthood existed to worship God in the Temple. That was its role. In support of that role, elaborate checks had been developed to determine just who was eligible to be a priest, or a High Priest. One of the rules was that your family must be able to produce a genealogy going back a number of generations, showing that your ancestors were of pure blood. These genealogies were kept in archives in the Temple and in major cities like Sepphoris, the capital of Galilee.

Within 40 years of Jesus' death, during the first of two wars between the Jews and the Romans, the Temple was destroyed. It was never rebuilt. In the course of the two wars (66-70 CE and 135 CE), the genealogical archives on which the priesthood depended were also destroyed. These two events made it impossible to revive a legitimate priesthood.

One could easily draw the conclusion that the God of history had acted to terminate the priesthood of the People of God. Meanwhile, what do the Catholics do? They decide that the old Israel had been superseded (poor theology at best) and that the Catholics are the New Israel. And if the Jews had a priesthood, as the new Christians discovered by reading the Jewish Scriptures, the church should have one, too. Besides, the ancients loved their priesthoods. The Greeks and the Romans had many of them. It was the most natural thing in the world for the new Roman Christians to set up their own priesthood to compartmentalize and administer their religious business. Administration and governance, after all, were the Romans' forte.

It was the work of perhaps a century and a half—from the mid-second century to the fourth century, in fact—to fit together all of the pieces and come up with an ideology that would justify and give employment to a Catholic priesthood. This effort of conscious and unconscious imitation first excluded women from the leadership positions they had previously held and then gave ownership and supervision of all Catholic religious practices to the male priesthood. At the end

---

[4] All of the Letter to the Hebrews, but especially Hb 7:23-27.

of this historical movement, the Roman talent for imperial administration had provided succeeding generations of the church with monarchical rule through a male priestly administration—a hierarchy.

That's why we have a male Catholic priesthood and monarchical clerical leadership in the Catholic church today— because it suited the cultural climate of the second and third centuries. It does not suit the cultural climate of the twentieth and twenty-first centuries. Even in the early days of the church, it was not unheard of that Catholics should vote for their bishops. The first letter of Clement testifies to that. But the present fossilized structure is wrong.

Jesus Christ did not die on the cross to preserve the cultural values of the Roman Empire. He did not die on the cross to preserve the Jewish priesthood—or any priesthood. That was our choice. And we can choose to change it. The most advanced nations in the world have seen the shortcomings of dictatorship, tyranny, absolute monarchy, and fascism in any form. We in the Catholic church can certainly take the same lesson from the God of history.

Rule by authoritarian fiat in the Catholic church hurls anathemas at the very God who placed the Holy Spirit in every human heart and mind. We have one Father in heaven and one Lord and teacher of us all, Jesus Christ. And the Spirit within us tells us whom to obey and who the hirelings and false shepherds are.

A simple proof of all of this is that the pope and the bishops are self-elected. They have created a walled city in the midst of the church. Only clergy may enter, and only clergy may vote—when they permit a vote. The rest of the church, the so-called "laity," remain outside, unconsulted and ineligible for leadership in the church. This two-tier Catholicism has a theological name. It is called schism, from the Greek, *schisma*— that which is torn in two, a division. It is a sin against unity, and it invalidates the claim of the "hierarchy" to leadership in the Catholic church, because they have set themselves apart from us.

In practice, priesthood is a cult of superiority. In their training, priests are encouraged to think of themselves as "other

Christs." This vitiates St. Paul's idea of the church as the Mystical Body of Christ, with the whole assembly of the faithful mystically continuing the presence and work of Christ in the world.[5] If only the priests are other Christs, then, to use Paul's phrase, Christ is divided up.[6]

And the pope's title, "the vicar of Christ," is downright blasphemous. As if the pope is the sole incarnation of Christ on earth! What does that assertion do to the theology of the real presence of Christ in the Eucharist, or the real presence of Christ in the assembly, the body of the church?

The hierarchy have acted as the caretakers of the rest of the church, as if we were minor children incapable of making decisions for ourselves. They have taken away the freedom of the children of God won for us by Jesus on the cross and instead have substituted an imperial papacy. But as in the children's story, this emperor has no clothes.

The Mass, the papacy, and the priesthood. What else can I criticize? It sounds as if I should go and join a church where these ideas would be more congenial. My reply? This is my church. I am a committed Catholic. I have been delving into the origins of the Catholic church for more than 50 years. I have attended weekly and sometimes daily Mass willingly all my life. My understanding and respect for this church and for the many priests I have known has increased enormously over the years. I will match my commitment with the pope's commitment to the church at any time. But in the matter of church structure and governance, the pope and his allies are in error. They are committed to a man-made organization, not to Jesus Christ. In my opinion, the pope's commitment to Christ, in this one respect, is defective. And so, quite seriously, the pope should leave the church before I do. Otherwise, he should forsake his mistaken commitment to a false authoritarianism that sets the values of his caste above the good of the faithful.

Don't misunderstand me. I know the Roman Catholic church's religious practices took years to develop and have been persisted in

---

[5] 1 Cor. 12:27; Eph. 1:22,23 and throughout Paul's letters
[6] 1 Cor. 1:13

for centuries. But Catholics cannot avoid the duty of examining new evidence when it comes to light. It is the work of Christian scholars that has created the exciting field of Christian origins. Their patient study, especially over the past century and a half, has revealed much that is new, knowledge that has greatly clarified our understanding of how the church came to be.

Catholics have been in the front ranks of these scholars for the last 50 years. Thus, almost everything I have learned in this field has come from priests. [I trust priests to understand the Catholic background.] A list of their names would include most of the leading Catholic Scripture scholars of the twentieth century and a number of Catholic theologians. However, because the Catholic church is not now a free society, I am very reluctant to name any of those scholars who are living, and I cite few passages from their works. To do so could invite reprisals.

Instead, I try to keep my arguments grounded in Scripture and in historical fact.

For those who see enormous difficulties in changing the religious practices of the Catholic church to agree more closely with gospel values—doing away with the papacy, substituting a more democratic form of church government, and sunsetting the priesthood *as the sole proprietor of Catholic religious practices, especially including the Mass*—let me tell you a true story. I believe it shows the direction in which the Holy Spirit is taking the church.

More than 40 years ago, in 1967 when the first reforms of Vatican II were beginning to be implemented, the Archdiocese of Chicago launched a campaign to better acquaint Catholics with the nature and origins of the Mass. For this effort, it selected teams of lay people in each parish to visit the homes of parishioners and show a filmstrip presentation called, "History of the Mass."

Ed Tryba and I were given one of these assignments. We entered the house and found a large living room with one long table in the center. About 20 people were seated and standing around the room. We didn't know the parishioners, so we introduced ourselves, explained what we were going to do, then set up the projector and the record-player, and began the filmstrip.

The presentation was well written and well illustrated. It took the viewer through five "episodes" in the history of the Mass from the Passover Meal to the Last Supper to the likely form of the Eucharist after the resurrection, i.e., the Sabbath meal, and then to the Mass as described by St. Justin, ca. 150 CE, and finally to the model of the Eucharistic Canon offered by Hippolytus, ca. 215 CE. The filmstrip left the people in reverential awe, their minds buzzing with ideas such as that, in the early days of the church, the celebrant made up his own Eucharistic prayer.

Ed and I did as instructed. We led the discussion connecting the five episodes. We asked people to recall other especially significant meals they had shared and to comment on the appropriateness of Jesus' choosing a meal by which to have his followers remember him. Finally, we asked people to compare Hippolytus's Eucharistic prayer with ours today. There were differences, but not substantial ones.

As instructed, we had all the people join hands around the long table and say the Our Father. Then we took an uncut loaf of bread from the table, broke it in pieces and gave each person a piece. Holding the pieces in our hands we all recited together, "We will know the Lord Jesus in the breaking of the bread."

As we ate the bread in silence, the hair on the back of my neck bristled as if with static electricity.

We were all in one room concentrating on the meaning of the Mass. We were all reflecting on the life of the Lord Jesus in prayer. And we were all recognizing the Lord Jesus in the breaking of the bread.

I didn't say a word to Ed Tryba about what I was feeling then. But after 40 years, almost every detail of that house church and that celebration is still etched in my memory. It was our first Mass as celebrants. Finally it makes sense to talk about it. The journey of a thousand miles begins with a single step.

Is this "talking treason" in the Catholic church? Or is it "a new birth of freedom" to which the Holy Spirit is calling us Catholics?

It seems high time to redefine the human constitution of the Catholic church along more democratic lines. If this be treason, let us make the most of it.

The first notion we must deal with, in this revolution to reform the Catholic church, is the idea that this church is not a democracy.

"The Church Is Not a Democracy".

This insult to lay Catholics is very common now. If you are interested in reforming the Catholic church, you have probably heard it more than once. Most recently, I heard it from the mouth of a bishop speaking to a group of Chicago Catholics–priests and lay parish leaders. It stuck in my craw. The bishop said it assertively, contemptuously, with full confidence that he would not be contradicted. And he was right. No one challenged that stupid statement.

Taken as a description of the Catholic church's current situation, however, it is painfully apparent that the church is not a democracy. The only opinion that counts in serious matters is the pope's. The pope in power as this is written chooses all of the world's Catholic bishops and seems determined to force his mindset onto the Catholic church throughout the world. The bishops do not contradict him. They don't want to see their careers sidetracked or terminated. The cardinals who head the Curia, the pope's court (royal court, not court of law), must be smiling amongst themselves. They have achieved their object. All of the voices of Vatican II have been silenced. The church is not a democracy, despite the democratic initiatives of its own most recent council.

But taken as a statement of historical or theological fact, the statement that the church is not a democracy is dead wrong. It marks those who use it as historical and theological ignoramuses.

In its earliest form after the death and resurrection of Jesus, the church was a brotherhood with a community of leaders, the apostles. Peter, by the way, was ONE of the leaders of this group, then centered at Jerusalem, not THE leader. THE leader who emerges in the Acts of the Apostles–contrary to the Lord's preference for Peter–was Jesus' brother, James, an early instance of church politics interfering with the will of God. Regardless, when the question arose about the daily distribution of food, the apostles did not want to deal with it. The Greek-speaking Jews who had brought the complaint were told, choose your own leaders to deal

11

with the problem. And the Greek-speaking community chose the first seven deacons.

Now, did they elect them? Probably not in our sense, through the use of a ballot box. But they most likely used a way even more democratic and more preferable–through consensus, in the style of a town meeting in which individuals called out names that were met with a murmur of assent from the group.

There are other examples of election by the laity in the early church:

The First Letter of Clement in the late first century (ca. 96 CE), despite its bias in favor of a church order that would imitate the Roman army, testifies to the custom of the laity electing leaders of the various churches.[7]

One of the strongest statements of the principle of election of bishops by the people is contained in the Apostolic Tradition of Hippolytus (ca. 215 CE):

> Let the bishop be ordained after he has been elected (chosen) by all the people. And when he has been proposed and found acceptable to all, the people shall assemble on the Lord's day together with the presbyters (elders) and such bishops as may be present. With the agreement of all (the people) let the bishops lay hands on him, and the presbyters stand by in silence.

In the fourth century, the Council of Nicaea (325 CE) and following councils enacted Canons omitting mention of and finally eliminating the vote of the laity from bishops' elections.

In the fifth century, pope St. Leo the Great (440-461 CE) was responsible for the statement with respect to bishops' elections, "He who governs all should be elected by all."[8] He didn't mean it in its full sense, however. Earlier he made a distinction between the clergy's electing a bishop, and the people's

---

[7] 1 Clem 44:3 "We do not think it just, then, to remove from their ministry those [bishops, overseers] who were appointed by them [the apostles], or later on by other eminent men, <u>with the consent of the whole church</u>..." Cf. also 1 Clem 54:1-2.

[8] Leo, *Epistles*, 10:6

"requesting" a bishop. Obviously the laity's ability to express their opinion in the church and be heard was eroding.

Finally, we should consider the election of St. Ambrose as bishop around 374 CE by the citizens of Milan. The clergy were gathered in the cathedral trying to decide which of their number, an Arian or a Catholic, to elect as bishop. The citizens present in the church, upset with the choices they faced, grew restive, and a riot seemed imminent. When Ambrose arrived as prefect of police to speak to the assembly, his words were so moderate, the citizens began chanting "Ambrose for bishop!" They forced his election, though he had not yet been baptized and was certainly not a priest.

This little anecdote reveals a turning-point in clerical-lay relations, the point at which the "professionals" began to assume complete control of the process. They didn't ask; they just took the prerogative away from the laity.

The emperors were already involved in the election of bishops. In fact, the clergy in the Milan cathedral offered the emperor Valentinian the choice of whom to appoint to the see of Milan. He refused, saying that the election should take place "in the usual way;" i.e., election by the people and approval by the clergy, including surrounding bishops. In later centuries, the emperors did assume the prerogative of naming local bishops and the pope as well. Only relatively recently in its long history has the hierarchical church freed itself from state control and only in modern times has the pope succeeded in acquiring the power of naming bishops throughout the world.

Today we are at another turning-point in clerical-lay relations. The hierarchy over the centuries have built up a nice little niche for themselves in the Catholic church. They are its rulers. If the popes had had their way during the Middle Ages, all the kings of Europe would have received their crowns from the pope as the supreme ruler on earth. The papacy was unsuccessful in this attempt. The princes of Europe were too powerful. Nevertheless, the hierarchy will not give up one iota of control over church matters to the laity–even if it means that thousands of Catholics in poorer countries must go without the benefits and consolations of the Mass and the sacraments. In fact, these hierarchs are acting very much the way George III acted toward the American colonies in the 18th century.

It seems time for a new Declaration of Independence. I was surprised at how easily the American Declaration of 1776 could be adapted to our present needs. See what you think:

A Declaration of Independence for the World's Catholics

When in the course of human events, it becomes necessary for an oppressed laity to dissolve the political bands which have subjected them to their hierarchical leaders, and to assume within the Catholic church, the equal and self-governing station to which the Laws of Nature and the Gospel entitle them, a decent respect to the opinions of humankind, especially of their fellow Catholics, requires that they should declare the causes which impel them to reject their present Government.

We hold these truths to be self-evident, that all men and women are created equal, that they are endowed by their Creator with certain unalienable Rights, that among these are Life, Liberty and the pursuit of Happiness. –That to secure these rights, Governments are instituted among human beings, deriving their just powers from the consent of the governed, –That whenever any Form of Government becomes destructive of these ends, it is the Right of the People to alter or to abolish it, and to institute new Government, laying its foundation on such principles and organizing its powers in such form, as to them shall seem most likely to effect their Safety and Happiness. Prudence, indeed, will dictate that Governments long established should not be changed for light and transient causes; and accordingly all experience has shown, that people are more disposed to suffer, while evils are sufferable, than to right themselves by abolishing the forms to which they are accustomed. But when a long train of abuses and usurpations, pursuing invariably the same Object evinces a design to reduce them under absolute Despotism, it is their right, it is their duty, to throw off such Government, and to provide new Guards for their future security. –Such has been the patient sufferance of the Catholic laity; and such now the necessity which constrains them to alter their former Systems of church Government. The history of the present Catholic hierarchy is a history of repeated injuries and usurpations, all having in direct object the establishment of an

absolute Tyranny over the Catholic church. To prove this let facts
be submitted to a candid world.

> They have built up the Catholic church as an
> absolute monarchy, ignoring the many instances of
> elections and other signs of democratic government
> that come to us from the early church, and ignoring,
> too, the strongly antihierarchical teaching of Jesus
> Christ when he said, "The greatest among you must
> be your servant."[9] In this, they have shown them-
> selves to be "pick-and-choose Catholics," picking
> as models for their administration the later, anti-
> democratic forms by which the church has been
> governed, instead of the earlier democratic forms.

> They have deprived Catholics of their birthright, the
> Mass, the very essence of the life of the church and
> the primordial sacrament that is its foundation, on
> the trivial ground that no one of the clergy approved
> by them is present as celebrant. They have thus
> denied to lay Catholics the right to celebrate Mass
> within their own homes, or wherever they choose,
> as Jesus requested and as the earliest Christians did.
> In this, they have acted directly against the life of
> the church.

> They are a self-perpetuating and self-appointed
> ruling class, never permitting Catholic lay people in
> the various dioceses or parishes to participate in any
> way in the selection or approval of any priest or
> bishop, but keeping entirely to the hierarchy and the
> clergy the choice of who should be a bishop or
> priest.

> They have failed totally to consult ordinary
> Catholics, the church-at-large, when deciding to de-
> clare a new doctrine or to commit the Catholic

---

[9] Mt 7:19

church to an important course of action, contenting themselves, if they speak to lay people at all, with seeking the opinions of friends or wealthy contributors, whose reactionary opinions they can count on to mirror their own.

They have laid heavy burdens on ordinary Catholics–through doctrines of their own manufacture, as in the Birth Control controversy–and they will not extend their little finger to lift them.

They have built up a huge superstructure of church government and have laid the faithful under heavy monetary contribution to support it, but they will not allow ordinary Catholics the least authority as to its governance.

They have followed a policy of covering up their administrative sins, as with priests not fit for the ministry who prey upon children or upon young adults by abusing them sexually; instead of removing such criminals from the priesthood, they have transferred them to other locations, sometimes without warning the churches to which they have been sent about their status as sexual predators.

They have committed a sin against the Holy Spirit by segregating the conduct and leadership of all the most important religious activities to a small portion of the church, namely: the clergy; binding them in allegiance to their hierarchical superiors through threats of nonsupport and promises of preferment; exacting penalties through silencings, removals, and withdrawals of faculties; demanding that they lead celibate lives; expecting that they wear distinctive clothing; teaching them that they are superior to the ordinary faithful; and, in every way possible, walling off the clergy from the great body of the church; and thus they have divided up the church, creating a yawning chasm between clergy and laity; and since the Holy Spirit inspires both clergy and laity, they have enforced schism within the Body of Christ for the sake of their own status and preferment.

They have propped up their own view of church governance by teaching lies, such as that Jesus Christ was a priest, when in fact he was a layman and seems to have been somewhat anticlerical (cf. the parable of the Good Samaritan); that Jesus ordained priests (no evidence in the New Testament); that St. Peter founded the Roman church and was the first pope (St. Peter died long before the monarchical episcopate came into being; the church had already been founded in Rome when Peter and Paul arrived, and Peter and Paul probably died because existing Roman church leaders, envying the Apostles' charismatic status, betrayed them to the Roman authorities); and atop all of this–the greatest lie of all–that Jesus commanded that the church have a hierarchical form of Government.

Through a refusal to reform their governing structure, they have set a terrible example for other Christians and for nations throughout the world; namely, that authoritarian and autocratic government which oppresses the people it governs is acceptable to God and a fit model to follow. They have thus exposed Catholics and others in the Third World to economic servitude, poverty, and the loss of human dignity, freedom, and life itself at the hands of fascist and otherwise authoritarian governments.

They have sought to impose a rigid class structure, like that of the Roman Empire, on the church that Jesus founded; and they have failed to extend to ordinary Catholics that respect for the Holy Spirit dwelling within them that begets trust, confidence, and holiness. In this, too, they have acted directly against the life of the church.

By concentrating the attention of the faithful upon their own hierarchy as the source of the religion of Jesus Christ, they have usurped the place of Jesus as the font of our knowledge of God; to the extent that they have succeeded, they have committed idolatry and caused others to do so.

They have enticed our children to enter the clergy, with meretricious claims of serving God, with the allure of time-honored ritual, and with the possibility of becoming "other Christs" and "ruling," as they see it, in Christ's stead; yet in training these young people, they have then bent them to serving the aims of hierarchical organization and the glorification of the institutional church.

They have quartered these clergy in houses and churches which we ordinary Catholics have built in our own neighborhoods and which we properly should be considered to own; but these clergy come as mercenaries owing everything to the hierarchy that created them and nothing to the great church of lay people which surrounds and supports them.

They have removed from bishops the power to deal with moral emergencies in their own dioceses, since, for instance, even the power to remove a predatory priest from the priesthood is a decision that must be referred to Rome; thus the hierarchy itself falls victim to its own nature, because the principle of hierarchy, carried to its inevitable conclusion, demands that every important decision must be referred to the monarch—in this case, the pope. This instance demonstrates most clearly how the hierarchical principle defeats the action of the

Holy Spirit in each and every person linked from lowest to highest in the chain of command.

They have hampered theologians who are priests or who teach in Catholic colleges or universities, demanding that such teachers receive the prior approval of the local bishop as to their appointment and putting whatever they teach or publish under the surveillance of the local bishop who may by his disapproval remove them from office. Thus they eliminate debate within the church–but only for people and institutions under their influence. Ordinary Catholics, it seems, are beneath their concern.

By their lies and political machinations, they have taken away the key to knowledge of the Kingdom of God; they themselves will not enter in and they will not permit others to enter in.

In every stage of these Oppressions We have Petitioned for Redress in the most humble terms: Our repeated Petitions have been answered only by repeated injury. A hierarchy whose character is thus marked by every act which may define a Tyrant, is unfit to lead a people who have the freedom of the Children of God.

Nor have We been wanting in attentions to our brethren in the Clergy. We have warned them from time to time of attempts by the Hierarchy to extend an unwarrantable jurisdiction over us. We have reminded them of the circumstances of our generations-long service to the Catholic church. We have appealed to their native justice and magnanimity, and we have conjured them by the ties of our common kindred to disavow these usurpations, which would inevitably interrupt our connections and correspondence. Some courageous ones have listened, putting their lives and careers on the line to help us, but most have been deaf to the voice of justice and of consanguinity. We must, therefore, acquiesce in the necessity, which demands our separation from hierarchical leadership, and hold the priesthood, as we hold the rest of humankind, Adversaries if they oppose us, but in agreement, Friends.

We, therefore, Representatives of the united Catholic people throughout the world Assembled, appealing to the Supreme Judge of the world for the rectitude of our intentions, do, in the Name, and by Authority of the Holy Spirit dwelling in the People of the Catholic church, solemnly publish and declare, That the Catholics of the world are, and of Right ought to be Free with the freedom that Christ came to bring us; that they are Absolved from all Allegiance to the Catholic Hierarchy, and that all political connection between them and the Catholic Hierarchy is and ought to be totally dissolved; and that as Free Children of God, they have full Power to baptize, to celebrate Mass, to confirm, to join in marriage, and to do all other Acts and Things which the Catholic church may of right do. And for the support of this Declaration, with a firm reliance on the protection of divine Providence, we mutually pledge to each other our Lives, our Fortunes and our sacred Honor.

* * * *

That's what a Declaration of Independence means. *That* is the freedom that Jesus Christ came to bring us. It means that we recognize that the church belongs to us, and we have the sobering responsibility to take back its powers when they have fallen into the wrong hands.

The problem is that the pope and the bishops who agree with him are blinded by presumption and by ignorance as to their own precarious position. They assume they are unassailable, that Jesus Christ gave them the church. This has made them arrogant. In their very arrogance lies their weakness.

I could have envisioned a much more fraternal middle course to solving this problem of authority in the Catholic church, but the history of the Roman church since Vatican I makes it clear that the pope and the bishops he creates will retain all ecclesiastical authority in their own hands, come hell or high water, and will not even think of sharing it.

That middle course would have seen a gradual unbundling and dissolution of the clerical state and a sharing of all clerical duties and responsibilities among the laity as need arose or occasion presented itself. It would have meant a revival of the laity voting for bishops and priests. Is there a "priest shortage" in Latin America or in Africa? Give Catholic lay people of good character and suitable inclination the responsibility of ministering in those areas and the training to do so properly. They would baptize, confirm, say Mass, marry, and anoint the sick wherever the need arose. They would act as they did in the early church. There is no lack of theological support for this kind of program. Are we not, as 1 Peter says, "a holy priesthood."[10] Of course, since the First Letter of St. Peter was written, we have given a whole new definition to what it means to be a priest. But each generation has its own insights, and we can take advantage of the best while we try to avoid the worst.

The great problem in the Catholic church today is not the priest shortage or even predatory priests, as horrific as that is. It is instead the division between the hierarchy and the great mass of the Catholic church and the paralysis that has fallen over the whole church as a result. The church has its hands tied by an authority that turns out to be false because it refuses to recognize the action of the Holy Spirit in the church.

If the Holy Spirit exists, it exists in every single member of the church. If the Holy Spirit exists, it enlivens every member of the church. If the Holy Spirit exists, it whispers the words of Jesus Christ to every member of the faithful. If the Holy Spirit exists, it gives the entire community the direction to do the work of Jesus Christ with a minimum of authoritarian control. If the Holy Spirit exists, it makes the church almost autonomous in its members. If the Holy Spirit exists, its members are likely to function best in a fairly loose democratic or mutually consensual structure.

More than that, if the Holy Spirit exists, it exists in all humankind, and God's revelation has not waited on our petty church squabbles to announce itself well in advance of our feeble proclamation to all the ends of the earth. Our duty, in obedience to the Holy Spirit, is to listen as well as to teach.

---

[10] 1 Pet. 2:5,9

The present order of the Catholic church is a total denial of all of this. Its leadership is unelected by the people; it is self-chosen; it is cut off from its roots in the Catholic people. It treats the Catholic people as "the simple faithful," who are unable to hear for themselves the promptings of the Holy Spirit and unable to understand the words of Jesus Christ–who certainly are incapable of carrying out any of the work of Jesus Christ in the world. It is a leadership that has built up a huge house of cards of philosophical approaches, theological approaches, words to say and not to say, rules to observe–not out of scripture but out of their own human tradition. All of which must be mastered before one can begin to do the work of Jesus Christ. They are deaf to the Holy Spirit.

As proof of that, neither Jesus Christ nor any of his disciples would qualify for leadership in the Catholic church as it is currently constituted. They would have too much to learn of "human precepts." And yet Jesus and his disciples were qualified to launch the greatest movement of lay religious reform in the history of the world–which only some centuries later became the Catholic church.

In any tree, the sap rises from the roots. But this seeming great tree of hierarchical leadership has already been cut off at the base. Its leaves are withering rapidly and falling off in great heaps. The next strong wind will send it crashing to the ground. The words of John the Baptist are coming true with a vengeance: "Every tree that does not bear good fruit will be cut down and thrown into the fire."[11]

We lay Catholics must think of the next generation. Many of our children have abandoned the Catholic church. And why not? It has no life. It needs a transfusion of Spirit. The hierarchy, believing that their place in the economy of salvation is an entitlement, feel that no action is required from them other than Not to Rock the Boat. They are Organization Men. They stopped listening to the Holy Spirit years ago. Any one of them who came up with Fresh New Ideas would lose his friends in the hierarchy and his employment. Every one of them is jammed together in the wheelhouse of the Titanic.

---

[11] Mt 7:19

It's up to us ordinary Catholics to save as many as possible of the hierarchy from themselves. Their ship, however, is a total loss. And the way we will set about that task of saving the church from the hierarchy is through Lay Catholic Renewal.

Lay Catholic Renewal

Lay Catholic Renewal is the same sort of movement in the Catholic church that Jesus Christ carried out in Israel. It is a movement of people without priestly or hierarchical distinction, a movement to renew their faith and the faith of the church in God. Lay Catholic Renewal takes positive action to renew the church by reviving the sacraments as practiced by the laity in the early church—long before there was a hierarchy—and by reviving charity as the most characteristic distinction of Catholic people. Lay Catholic Renewal forms base communities where ordinary people can meet to study, to celebrate the sacraments, and to develop inspired leaders for the church of the future. Lay Catholic Renewal does away with the hierarchical principle by recognizing hierarchy for what it is—an attack on the Holy Spirit. Hierarchy, in practice, denies the existence of the Holy Spirit in anyone but the hierarchs themselves. Hierarchy denies that the Holy Spirit resides and acts within each member of the church and in the church as a whole and that this same Spirit must be consulted and heeded in order for the church to succeed in its work.

Who is eligible to join in this movement of Lay Catholic Renewal?

Anyone. There is only one provision. He must be able to leave all of his hierarchical distinctions at the door. Certainly members of religious orders are eligible. Many of them have suffered greatly from hierarchy and generally have nothing to do with its distinctions. Priests and bishops are eligible—provided they are able to enter as a little child. [Oh, how Jesus' words come back to us and help us with this effort!] The church of the apostles had many converts who were also priests. None is recorded to have joined the early church from the ranks of the High Priestly families.

Lay Catholic Renewal will test the hearts and minds of many Catholics. It will ask them to reexamine what they believe and in whom they believe.

Basic Catholicism

If you were to ask any random group of Catholics what they consider to be the irreducible minimum of Catholicism–of what the Catholic faith consists at rock bottom–you would get a variety of answers. The answers might include some or all of the following: the Mass, the following of Jesus Christ, observance of the Ten Commandments, the sacraments, the priesthood, the papacy, the apostolic succession, prayer, veneration of the saints, veneration of the Blessed Mother, observance of the commandments of the church, works of charity, the corporal and spiritual works of mercy, their parish, their diocese, the real presence, the Mystical Body, the People of God, missionary work, the communion of the faithful, the Scriptures, Catholic tradition, the cardinal virtues, the theological virtues, yes, and even the hierarchy.

In past ages, this list might have included the divine right of kings and the condemnation of usury, that is: earning interest on money you lent to someone. But these ideas have been abandoned, even though they once loomed fairly large in rules of church observance.

What is basic Catholicism? As in so many areas, the Jews have been our precursors in answering religious questions like this. Judaism suffered a staggering setback when the Temple of Jerusalem was destroyed by the Romans in the First Jewish War (66-70 CE). Jerusalem lay in ruins. The country was filled with refugees from the war. For the Jews, an important focus of their religion, the Temple cult, which employed thousands of priests, Levites, and other religious workers, had simply disappeared.

This loss left an enormous gap in the religious observance of the Jewish people. Much of their life had revolved around the various pilgrimages to the Temple throughout the year. Passover (March-April) was foremost, but there were also other feasts–the Feast of Weeks (Pentecost, May-June) and the Feast of Booths (Sukkot, Sep-Oct), which were with Passover the three great pilgrimage feasts. There were also the Day of Atonement (Sep-Oct), the Feast of the Dedication of the Temple (Hanukkah, Dec), and the Feast of Purim (Feb-Mar). The Temple was felt to be the place where God dwelt on earth; it was felt to be the people's physical connection with God, where they could offer sacrifice and obtain forgiveness. The Jewish people, who were spread all over the world at that time, must have felt the Temple's loss profoundly.

In this emergency, a small group of religiously minded men gathered at Jamnia, intent on restoring the Jewish religion. The group probably consisted of various elements of the Jewish religious spectrum at that time–priests, Pharisees, religious scholars (scribes), and possibly even a few Sadducees, i.e., members of the former High Priestly families. In time, the descendents of this group would succeed in writing down many of the religious traditions about the Temple and religious practice that had never before been reduced to writing.

Their thought probably was directed toward an eventual rebuilding of the Temple. After all, this was not the first time the Temple had been destroyed. The Babylonians had destroyed the First Temple in 587 BCE. In fact, it was undoubtedly that first destruction of the Temple that gave rise to the synagogue. The loose network of synagogues survived the devastation of the Second Temple as well. Little more than local religious meeting-houses and schools, the synagogues became the focus of religious survival for the Jews. They eclipsed even the local priesthood, which still existed in the country places of Israel.

It was the synagogue service that filled the gap left by the loss of the Temple liturgy and filled religious needs no longer being met by the Temple. One aspect of the synagogue service worth mentioning was that the service could be held anywhere. The basic requirement was a minyan–ten men, none of whom needed any religious qualification other than being a Jew.

What Christians have, comparable to this kind of flexibility, is a word of the Lord: "Where two or three are gathered together in my name, I am in the midst of them" (Mt 18:20). Jesus' words come thick and fast supporting efforts to empower Catholic Christians: "I will ask the Father and He will give you another Advocate,...the Spirit of Truth.... [Y]ou know it, because it remains with you and will be in you. I will not leave you orphans." (Jn 14:16-18). And "The Advocate, the Holy Spirit that the Father will send in my name–he will teach you everything and remind you of all that I told you." (Jn 14:26) And "I came that (you) might have life and have it more abundantly." (Jn 10:10). What greater life is there than to come closer to the one who said, "I am the resurrection and the life. Whoever believes in me, even if he dies, will live." (Jn 11:25)

But to follow Christ as a Catholic imposes obligations. We cannot ignore the plight of the Catholic church and our part in remedying its situation. The shock you may have felt after reading the Catholic Declaration of Independence is similar to the shock the Jews felt at being deprived of their Temple. They couldn't know at the time that God was ending the priesthood of Aaron. But that historical fact should prepare us to see the needs of our own church in a new light.

Is it acceptable to drift along with the diminishing flow of Catholic church life, to watch parish schools close, parishes close, parish congregations decline while neighboring or distant evangelical or other churches swell with hundreds and thousands of former Catholics who no longer feel any nourishment for their spiritual lives within the Catholic church?

Is it acceptable to look around when parish-wide meetings are called and find that there are few if any present under the age of 35, that the median age of people with any interest left in the parish is probably 55 or 60?

Is it acceptable listening to sermons from a clergy who must maintain a barrier between themselves and the faithful, who are not really familiar with their parishioners' lives, and, at best, have not the authority to invite people into closer communion with the church or with Christ?

Is it acceptable to be asked for larger and larger contributions for maintenance of church property "on faith," when you know that huge amounts of money have been paid out in secret to victims of one kind of clerical abuse?

Is it acceptable in your own church to feel absolutely powerless to affect policies that you know in your own mind are wrong?

Is there an alternative? Yes! But it IS radical. It is as radical as the threat that Jesus Christ posed to the priesthood of his time. He carried on the work of his Father with a careful wariness of their establishment, their rules, and their bullying tactics. They saw him as a threat, and they were right! He was a threat. They killed him, colluding with the Roman government to get the job done.

And within 40 years, the Temple and that entire priesthood were destroyed.

There were signs to be seen at that time, too, and that priesthood didn't see them. The wind was blowing, and they could not reckon its strength or its direction. They had no idea Whom it was that they opposed.

* * * *

Essential to the Catholic faith is the following of Jesus Christ through constant prayer, the Mass, Baptism, and the other sacraments, and the corporal and spiritual works of mercy, what the Jews call 'acts of loving-kindness.' You can't do that intelligently without studying the scriptures and understanding them through good teachers or good works of commentary. Along with that is the *koinonia*, i.e., the 'brother-and-sisterhood,' the fellowship, what we have come to call the 'communion of the faithful.'[12] Then comes the preaching of the Kingdom of God. Included in all of this is a recognition that the movement that Jesus Christ founded was inclusive, not exclusive. It tended to bring people in, not cast them out. Though protective of its values, it was not judgmental. It had porous boundaries. It aimed at the unity of all humankind, all of whom are God's children. It respected the insights of other cultures and was willing to learn from them, recognizing that the Holy Spirit of Jesus Christ has already preceded us throughout the world. As he said, "I have other sheep that do not belong to this fold. These also I must lead...." (Jn 10:16)

On the other hand, everything of what people may believe to be essential to the Catholic faith that has to do with governance, or rule, is a historical accretion, a human invention. It is highly suspect. Many Catholics believe that what they have been taught about governance is part of the "deposit of faith," in other words something that must be believed because it was given to us by Jesus Christ. They believe this because they have been taught so

---

[12] In modern times, this notion has been adopted in secular society as the 'community.'

from their infancy. But what they have been taught about church governance is false.

To the extent that the hierarchy <u>know</u> that what they teach about church governance is false, they lie. Hierarchy, priesthood, papacy–and theories like apostolic succession that have been used to prop them up–all are part of the current government's power structure. It doesn't matter how many centuries they have held sway. They have all been used to control the faithful and deprive them of their heritage. They are works of man and not of God. They lack force and validity and, in fact, are all repealed here and now. Everything else remains.

And if the hierarchy ask us by whose authority we do these things, we will ask them to tell us first about the laity's election of leaders in the early church–was it from God or from human beings? No matter which way they answer, their case is lost. For if they say, 'It was from God,' we are vindicated. And if they say, 'It was from human beings,' then so were all of the self-appointments of popes, bishops, and other clergy–and they all may be changed by human beings. And again we are vindicated. Remember, Jesus was a layman. He had no official standing in the church of his time, either.

Even God has his seasons. Even God acts in the fullness of time. God sent his son at a certain time, but the leaders then did not recognize him. It is foolish for us now to act as if time has no ripeness, no seasons. As if everything that now exists has always existed and must remain unchanged. The fact is that the Catholic church has undergone cosmic changes, decade by decade, from the time of its birth. Almost nothing now is as it was in the past. Our world-view is different, our understanding of ourselves and of God is different from the world-view and understanding of people in the past. Only God, the Son of God, and the Holy Spirit remain the same. It is an odd trick of history that we today, 2,000 years after the birth of Christ, have more resources at our disposal to study the time of Christ than did St. Clement in the year 96 CE when he wrote the letter sent on behalf of the church of Rome to the Corinthian church, which was then in turmoil.

Clement speaks of the holy apostles going about, "with perfect foreknowledge," appointing leaders of the various churches they founded. We know now that they did no such thing. They had no "perfect foreknowledge." And, St. Paul being the clearest example of a missionary apostle presented to us in the New Testament, we must draw the conclusion from his career that, for the most part, the apostles did not appoint leaders of their own choosing, but accepted existing leaders in the churches they founded. Clement, in one respect, was at an incredible disadvantage compared with us today. The New Testament had not yet been put together. It existed only as scattered writings treasured in the various churches. Clement knew the Jewish scriptures, which were somewhat more available in Greek translations, but his knowledge of all the writings that now compose the New Testament left a great deal to be desired. What he gives us, however, is the valuable tradition that Peter and Paul were both put to death in Rome and on account of "unrighteous zeal"–the envy probably of Jewish Christian missionaries insistent that gentile converts be circumcised who looked on Peter and Paul as troublemakers (1 Clem. V:4).

Each age of the church must solve the problem it faces. Ours is the problem of an overreaching and inept hierarchy that is strangling the life out of the church. We must not let that happen. We can have church government that is accountable to the people– and to the Holy Spirit. It can be WITH the present leaders, if they agree to stand for election and agree to a full accounting and full transparency of all of their actions. It will be WITHOUT the present leaders if they insist on defending their supposed privileges.

If we are able to act WITH the cooperation of the present leaders, we can save much of the church's heritage of historic manuscripts, art and architecture, institutions such as the Vatican Library, and other important repositories of past history. If we must act WITHOUT the present leadership–and they choose to further alienate the laity on whom they depend–much of those artifacts may be sold off by the present hierarchy to pay the cost of their ongoing expenses.

No one wants to see that happen. But if this serious movement to renew the church results in a conflict between the Old Guard and an insurgent Catholicism which will no longer tolerate the hierarchy's version of the divine right of kings, we may be compelled to set up a shadow government alongside the existing and discredited government. This may be expensive. It may well take much of the funds previously allocated to existing church structures.

This dark prospect must be faced. It is like the view that Jesus had when he wept over Jerusalem. His too, like ours, was a generous and simplistic view–that those who disagreed with him could somehow be reconciled to him, because he was indeed the prophet who was to come. For us the situation is different, but similar. We are Jesus' church. We hear his voice as well as the hierarchy does and probably better, considering that we do not feel invested in a creaking totalitarian bureaucracy that weighs like a millstone around the neck of the church itself.

For too long, now, the Official Catholic Church has vehemently rejected any possibility that the laity ought to share in governing the Catholic church. The Lord has permitted them to be consumed by their own arrogance. God has humiliated them in the shame of their own sins. He has closed their mouth. They have nothing to say. Now, unless the hierarchy are able to divest themselves of all of the governmental baggage they carry and join with the laity on an equal footing, ONLY the voice of the laity can save the Official Catholic Church from its sins.

This is the insight that prompts the Lay Catholic Renewal movement.

Of course, we are talking politics here. The government of the church is <u>purely political</u>. To the extent that it succeeds in carrying out Christ's mandate to teach all nations, it transforms the political into the sacred. To the extent that it fails and attempts to <u>rule</u> the laity and all nations in sacred matters, it remains purely political and is subject to removal and replacement, as now.

First Steps in Lay Catholic Renewal

All politics is local. Each of us has an opportunity to make the Kingdom of God come alive in his or her own neighborhood. Each of us in our own parish can cooperate in setting up a group–a base community–that will, by its very existence, begin the effective reform of the church. This group will have several functions:
- To spread news of the Lay Catholic Renewal movement's agenda and activities in the local parish, through meetings with

the pastor and assistants (if any), through parish meetings, and through the formation of base communities within the parish
- To recapture the sacramental life of the church from the grasp of the hierarchy through the celebration of home Masses conducted by the faithful in the base communities
- To increase the faithful's understanding of the church by serious study of the church's history and theology, especially the Scriptures
- To reach out to nearby Catholic parishes and religious communities to spread the message of Lay Catholic Renewal as a first step to building a broader organization
- To be prepared to send representatives to municipal, state, or national meetings, if called on to do so, to report on and represent the activities of your parish group
- To encourage each member of a base community to set up a separate bank account for possible contributions to the Catholic church renewal movement

Here is a brief sketch of the rationale for these points:

Relations with Your Own Parish

In the best of all possible worlds, your relations with your local parish are good now and will remain good even after your status as a Lay Catholic Reformer becomes known and understood. That may be too much to hope for. The clergy may think that our objective is to put them out of business. Not so. Our view is that they are rapidly putting themselves out of business–with the aid of the Holy Spirit–and our concern is to prevent the Catholic church from going down with them. We believe that the formation of a Catholic priesthood was an understandable mistake of history. All of the societies in which Christianity took its first roots had priesthoods: Israel, Egypt, Greece, and Rome. The priest in those societies was the religious "professional." Most often, his (or her) job was to preside over the ritual and maintenance of a temple. He or she was thought to be in the service of a god.

We count the Jewish priesthood as a special case. Judaism was and is a true religion. We believe God has a special relationship with the Jewish people and that we owe the authenticity of our religion to the fact that theirs is a true religion, and we draw our origin from their faith in the one, true God. This is what makes it profoundly significant that WE follow THEIR Messiah, even though they, when he came, did not accept him; that their Messiah acted as a layman who challenged and was put to death by their priesthood; and that their priesthood, which was set up by God, was abolished by what looks like an act of God 40 years after the death of Jesus Christ.

The New Testament knows of no Catholic priesthood. It tells us, however, that the Eucharist was celebrated in house churches–obviously by lay people. It is <u>certain</u> that people were not <u>ordained</u> to celebrate the Eucharist. Paul, who founded churches, complains about the improper celebration of the Eucharist by different groups within a house church (1 Cor 11:17-29). Obviously, these groups were not ordained to celebrate the Eucharist. They were acting in response to the Lord's command–but without proper respect. We intend to respond to the same call, but with proper respect. And the present clergy are welcome to join us as part of the Church in Renewal–not, however, as its rulers and lawmakers.

In these endeavors, parish facilities should be open to us who support the parishes. If they are not, that's regrettable, but it should not cause us either to fail in building base communities nor to cease supporting facilities occupied by the clergy. In the best outcome, all of these facilities will be saved, or at least disposed of in the manner most conducive to Catholic church Renewal.

All this, however, is by way of background. The concrete question is, How are you to approach your particular parish situation? The answer is, Let the Holy Spirit be your guide. For most people, the best initial approach will be to let the publicity that is likely to precede this movement do the work for you. The next step will be to put some form of this publicity in the hands of your parish clergy and ask for their cooperation. Make sure, though, that the movement is not misrepresented. We are not looking for conflict but for cooperation.

Recapturing the Sacramental Life of the Church

We will be a more thoroughly Catholic people when we ourselves celebrate the sacramental life of the church instead of delegating that activity to others. As in all things, we must take Jesus Christ as the model of our behavior. Reviving the celebration of the Mass by the laity will be one of the hallmarks of Lay Catholic Renewal. When Jesus and his disciples were gathered in the upper room for what would be the Last Supper, Jesus did not send out to the Temple for a priest to officiate at the ritual he was inaugurating. The idea is ludicrous, right? The absolute novelty of what Jesus was doing has always escaped us because of little arguments that whisper to us mentally and add subtle qualifications to what we read in the New Testament. Arguments such as:

- Well, Jesus did not need a priest because he was much greater than a priest. He was the Son of God. He was the savior of the world. He was, in effect, the first priest of the new order.
- Besides, the Jewish priests were not the same kind of priests as Catholic priests. They had to do with the Temple ritual, not with the Catholic Mass.

Both of these objections are freighted with the accumulated weight of later history and later interpretation. This history and interpretation have to be stripped away in order to see clearly what Jesus was doing. Jesus did not approach his disciples as anything other than a human being, a layman without religious distinction except that he very much resembled an ancient prophet. Not a priest. It was his actions that spoke for him. Yet there was a similarity between what Jesus was doing at the Last Supper and the sacrifices being prepared in the Temple for that Passover. So the idea of calling in a priest is not utterly without merit.

He could have called in a priest. He didn't do so. The effect was to bring the new ritual completely home to people. To put it in their midst and in their hands. You didn't need an imposing Temple to carry out this ritual. And you did not need a special representative of the people to carry it out. It was something you did together, a joint celebration, a communion. Obviously, Jesus would dominate any gathering of which he was a part. But at the Last Supper, his natural spirits were failing him. He was emotionally down. He was the presider, as the term now is, but less a presider and more a simple participant, with others dipping their bread in the bowl of wine at the same time as he did.

The Mass does not belong to the priests. Years elapsed in the process, but the plain fact is, they took it away from us. For years, Mass was conducted in some parts of the Western and the Eastern churches as if it was purely a matter between the priests and God. As early as the fourth century, after the victory of Constantine, when large churches began to be built, a line of division was drawn between the clergy and the laity. In the Western church, this line was signified by a low screen or fence between the sanctuary or *presbyterium* (clergy's place) and the nave of the church where the laity stood. The line of demarcation took many forms. It often extended into the nave of the church as the number of clergy swelled. Sometimes the low screen became a high screen, as in the Eastern church, and occasionally it became a solid wall on two sides. In recent years in most Western churches, the division between clergy and laity was reduced to an altar rail and then, after the Second Vatican Council, the altar rail was finally removed. For centuries, the priest turned his back on the people; the idea was that both priest and people would face east, but everyone including the priest got the impression that the priest was alone with God. He uttered the prayers of the Mass silently, only occasionally raising his voice. The need for mystery came to be considered important; the need to share the rite with the people was not. And we lay people, not understanding what was going on, not understanding our own position and our own rights, and willing to trust the professionals, acquiesced in the takeover.

Some of us are fully alert now. We are willing to take a long look at the history of the Mass, recognize its essence, and return it to the more simple, more powerful union of ourselves with Christ and with his Father that it was intended to be. We will have more to say about how to celebrate Mass later on. For now, it is enough to point out that the question of whether women should say Mass is entirely mooted by this movement of Lay Catholic Renewal. Women were among the earliest Christians to celebrate the Eucharist. Now, finally, they can do so again.

As to the other sacraments, the most important after the Eucharist is Baptism. It has for long been a matter of Catholic doctrine that "in an emergency" any lay person may baptize a child. This rule was used to invidious effect by Pope Pius the Ninth when he had a Jewish boy abducted from his parents and raised as a Catholic because the boy had been baptized by the family's maid.

So everyone agrees that lay people may validly baptize. A concern for us will be to have the Baptisms properly registered. The ease with which we today can create large databases will simplify this task.

The other sacraments are creations of the church and are of less importance to the life of the church, though they are useful in bringing us closer to God–with one exception. That one exception, of course, is Ordination. That particular sacrament has been used as a tool by the existing Catholic church government. As part of the hierarchy's method of maintaining its leadership in the church, it is highly suspect. When the church is fully renewed, Ordination will be used as a way of signifying only that a leader has been delegated by the Catholic people, acting in the Holy Spirit, to perform a certain office for a given term, and no more than that. I am sure that God will see that the laying on of hands by the authority of the faithful in the power of the Holy Spirit is attended by as many graces as in the past, and perhaps more.

A word about the idea of Apostolic Succession, which the hierarchy have used to insure their control of church leadership. In the early days of the church, bishops used to dispute among themselves about whose see (i.e., seat of church government) was the greater and more authentic and whose see was lesser and should be subject to a greater see. (Governance again.) They came up with the idea that a local church, in order to be authentic, had to be able to trace its foundation back to one of the apostles. This led to a flurry of mythmaking about which apostles founded what churches. That's probably how St. James, in mythic tradition, managed to travel to Spain, where his tomb is now located, when St. Paul, in all likelihood, never reached that country, though he very much wanted to go there.

In the process, these episcopal theorists also developed the idea that if any bishop could not establish that he was validly ordained by a bishop who was also validly ordained, and so on, going back to one of the apostles, he was not entitled to his post. This led to the formation of rules about what was and was not a valid ordination.

This is nonsense. It is totally unverifiable. In answer to this kind of mumbo-jumbo, I think St. John the Baptist would have said that God can create bishops out of these stones–if he wanted bishops in the first place. The answer of the Catholic people is to test their leaders themselves. If they want to continue to call them bishops, well and good. But the validity of their election depends upon the Holy Spirit and not upon some far-fetched human rationalization of an unbroken mythic chain.

Understanding Church History and Theology–Especially the Scriptures

To sustain the Lay Catholic Renewal movement, we will have to devote time to serious study. We ought to know at least as much about the history of the Catholic church as the average church official, and preferably more. Even more important is the study of the Scriptures. Our object is to understand the life of Jesus Christ in its historical context and to draw our theological conclusions from that understanding.

The last 50 years have given us a wealth of well researched studies of the life of Christ, the early church, and the Scriptures– many of them by Catholic scholars. The later history of the church swells to a far wider topic, encompassing as it does almost all of European history for the last 2000 years. There are far fewer compendious sources for this vast history that, nevertheless, preserve the sense of 'what happened' during each age of the church and 'what it meant' for subsequent church history. Later on in this book, however, you will find a brief bibliography of sources for study of the Scriptures, the life of Christ, the early church, and the church after the age of the apostles, i.e., the historical Catholic church. Please make yourselves as familiar with these works and with the Scriptures as you can.

Why is conscientious study so important? The short answer is, Because "the truth will set you free." We lay people lament and wring our hands over the scandals in the Catholic church, over (some few) priests committing heinous crimes against young people, while an even greater number of bishops and their staffs and counselors scurry around covering up the misdeeds, transferring the predators from place to place, swearing the victims to secrecy, and paying huge amounts of parishioners' contributions to ensure the cover-ups. The hierarchy compound the crimes. They have lost their moral compass. They have forgotten the gospel. They have abandoned Christ. They ought to be ousted! And yet because we do not yet understand the full sense of Christ's life and later church history, we do not realize that we have, not just every right, but full power to root these ecclesiarchs and their aiders and abettors out of their offices.

I am reminded of the fresh wind that blew through the church when Vatican II was in session. One man, John XXIII, succeeded in opening some of the windows at least part way, and the breeze that blew then was very refreshing. The windows have been slammed shut by the Curia[13] now, lo, these many years. But one story typifies the effect that a little knowledge of church history can have. As I heard the story, at the time of Vatican II a Benedictine liturgical scholar found himself at a meeting of Canon lawyers. The discussion turned to the subject of Baptism and the requirements for a valid Baptism. The Canonists reached a consensus that no Baptism could be considered valid unless at least enough water was poured on the head of the person to be baptized so that it would trickle. This would preserve the idea of washing the newly baptized clean of his or her sins.

"Then for at least 10 centuries of the church's history, no Baptism was valid," said the Benedictine, "because they were all done by aspersion," that is, by sprinkling.

I cannot vouch for the accuracy of the story, but that's the way it was told to me 40 years ago.

John Henry Newman, later Cardinal Newman, wrote a work of path-breaking scholarship before he came to eminence in the Catholic church. His study was *The Arians of the Fourth Century*. It aroused a controversy because it seemed to say that the entire Catholic church hierarchy–all of the bishops and the pope–became Arians for a period of 60 years under the influence of Roman emperors who were Arians, only to be saved from this heresy by the faithful, who remained Catholic in spite of what they were hearing from the pulpit.

---

[13] The pope's royal court, the Vatican bureaucracy.

Newman's book did not sit well with certain nineteenth century Roman prelates. Their arrogant assertion was that the faithful can know nothing which they have not received from above, from their teachers, the bishops. People began explaining away what Newman wrote. So in later editions of the book, which was a best-seller as works of religious scholarship go, Newman added an appendix that underlined the role of the faithful in saving the church from heresy in the fourth century. It was entitled, "On Consulting the Faithful in Matters of Doctrine."

In this work of historical theology, Newman disproved the notion that the Holy Spirit necessarily works in a 'trickle-down' fashion from the *magisterium* (the bishops in their teaching function, the so called *ecclesia docens*, the 'teaching church') to the simple faithful (the so called *ecclesia discens*, the 'learning church'). He proved that, during the fourth century, the Holy Spirit worked up from the grass roots, not down from the top.

These two anecdotes illustrate, I hope, how much better it is for us as reformers to know as much as possible about the church–and more than our seemingly entrenched church "leaders." They profess to believe a myth about the church's founding that is just not true. Much of our work will consist in digging people's heads out of the sand. And for that we need the tools of scholarship. The Holy Spirit will see that our words are not uttered without effect.

Spreading the Message of Lay Catholic Renewal to Neighboring Parishes and Religious Communities

If we can make inroads in our own parish, spreading the message of Lay Catholic Renewal to neighboring parishes and other religious communities should be easy. In an odd way, we are in fact reliving the very earliest age of the church. The task that Jesus' disciples faced was to convince their Jewish brethren that Jesus was indeed the Messiah, the Promised One. To accomplish this task, individual churches sent "apostles" to other communities and the synagogues in these communities, to establish communities of believers in the Messiah (Christ) and to nourish the communities that had been founded. In exactly this fashion, St.

Paul urged the church in Rome to welcome the (woman) apostle Phoebe into their midst before he himself was able to go to Rome.

It will be important for us to cross-pollinate our various communities, sending people wherever they are needed to explain the Lay Catholic Renewal movement, encouraging and instructing people in Scripture, history, and sacramental life, and on the mechanics of not letting the movement grow stale. If the salt loses its savor, then the bad guys win. But more of that later on. In the early days of the church, this work was done by individual communities, anxious to share the joy of the Resurrection and prepare people with whom they had ties for the imminent return of the Lord. It was an urgent matter for them. We should take on this task with the same urgency. This is our way of sharing in the Resurrection of Christ and his church. Besides, in all seriousness, who knows when the Lord may return. Better not to find us napping.

The Lay Catholic Renewal movement will discern its own leaders. It is important that they be in the mold of Peter and Paul and not of the current leadership, who are, by design, autocrats. The early church had its share of personality conflicts, as well as conflicts in teaching. I hope succeeding ages have taught us something about avoiding unnecessary conflicts. At some stage, however, it may be important to form something like a coordinating committee and adopt a plan of action. The Internet will be a great help in keeping people informed and in tracking the progress of reform. A number of lay Catholic organizations have websites that will help to speed the process.

To be prepared to send representatives to municipal, state, or national meetings, if called on to do so, to report on and represent the activities of your parish group

To encourage each member of a base community to set up a separate bank account for possible contributions to the Catholic church renewal movement

The last two points are self-explanatory. They embody the idea of setting up an organization within the Catholic church that will be accountable to the Church-at-Large, the laity. The second point is an attempt to safeguard people against fraud and corruption by keeping their contributions safe in their own pockets until they feel enough confidence in an authentic leadership to offer their monetary support.

It is difficult to see what forms the Lay Catholic Renewal effort will take. Whatever happens, funds may be required for city, state, or national meetings, for example, or for charitable works of various kinds. In the United States, where the church is not state-supported as it is in some European countries, Catholics are among the poorest contributors to their church of any religious group. That is probably to be explained by the total lack of accountability of the hierarchy to the laity and their habit of not listening to the laity. Nevertheless, it is an important sign of commitment to contribute to religious causes. In fact, those who tithe tend to feel much more commitment than those who contribute little.

I would recommend that each member of a base community (1) continue your regular parish contribution and (2) open a separate bank account in your own name with another family member or trusted friend as co-signer and begin "contributing" to that account an amount of money each week that will make up the difference between what you already contribute to the clerical church and one-tenth of your income. This fund will be available at your discretion for the church renewal effort. I would not recommend that any base community set up a common fund. We don't want to create any Judases–or Ananiases.

It is important that control of the renewal movement remain at the grassroots level. By keeping the funding in the pockets of those who furnish it, we avoid a lack of accountability similar to the one we complain of. Funds will be dispensed as a result of individual decisions to support the proposals of delegates.

What Our Attitude Should Be

In launching the Lay Catholic Renewal movement, we should go "as sheep among wolves." We must be "wise as serpents, simple as doves."[14] We do not wish to blame anyone for the current situation. It is perhaps not entirely the fault of the current leaders

---

[14] Mt. 10:16

that they don't understand how the church arrived at its present situation or what a false position they occupy in the light of the gospel and subsequent church history. They have been beguiled by their own press notices. Any autocratic organization creates sycophants who do nothing but praise the leader and the organization that keeps him in power. This extends even to the Fathers of the church. They have to be read carefully and with a good understanding of the influence exerted on them by the times in which they lived. We don't accept their anti-Semitism; neither should we accept their ideas of monarchical governance. The church has had powerful bad examples to lead it astray. Chief among them was the Roman Empire which, in many respects, gave birth to Roman church organization. Then there is the myth of Parmenides, the idea that nothing ever really changes, that "Things have always been this way and always will be." This is a counsel of despair. Society can improve, if only slowly and painfully, with a great deal of self-sacrificing labor. Without that labor it can also grow worse. Life is what you make it.

Be thankful you do not live at the time of Giordano Bruno or Galileo Galilei or the countless thousands who suffered under the Inquisition. At the same time, we must be wary. The current scandals in the priesthood have been enabled and exploited by corrupt bishops. There is no telling how deep that corruption goes or what it is capable of. Jesus did not trust himself to his enemies until he was ready to undergo martyrdom. And we know what the priesthood of his time did to him.

In addition, religion is one of those areas in our lives, like language, that tend to go unexamined. We take it for granted, probably because it's a part of our upbringing and our personality. If someone criticizes the way we speak or the way we worship God, we feel deeply offended without really understanding why. That's one of the reasons why church reform is so difficult. It upsets people at the core of their being. We for our part must remain patient, respectful of others, willing to explain, and confident that God will help us to a successful outcome.

But the most profound change in Catholic practice that Lay Catholic Renewal will revive from the church's earliest history is the celebration of Mass by lay people in their own homes. It will also be the most potent weapon in disassembling the false hierarchy that pretend to be our governors. Let us now examine how we got the Mass as it is now practiced.

What are the essentials of the Mass? The story of the two disciples on the road to Emmaus on Easter Sunday (Lk 24: 13-35) gives us an insight. The disciples are journeying the seven miles from Jerusalem to Emmaus, discussing the events of the past weeks. They are downcast. Jesus draws alongside them, but they do not recognize him. They are astounded that he does not know of the events they are discussing. Then he begins to explain the scriptures to them, pointing out all the passages that show that it was necessary for the Messiah to suffer before entering his glory. They come to a wayside inn where they plan to spend the night. Jesus makes as if to go on, but they persuade him to come in with them. They sit down to eat. Jesus takes the bread, says the blessing, breaks it, and offers it to them. The eyes of the disciples are opened. They recognize Jesus in his characteristic action, and he vanishes. They rush back to Jerusalem to tell the brothers and sisters. Their comment to one another is, "Were not our hearts burning within us when he spoke to us on the road and opened the scriptures to us?" At the close of the story, Luke underlines the fact that Jesus was made known to them "in the breaking of the bread."

That was very probably a Mass. Two or three people, the minimum. A breaking open of the scripture so that its meaning comes alive. And a sharing in the table of fellowship with the Lord. The result: a ridiculous, amazing joy. "We have seen the Lord! He is alive! He is not dead!" The earliest Christians would have seen this as an object lesson in celebrating the Mass.

Let us back up. Let's go back to Jesus in his earthly life, before the Resurrection, when he was in the midst of his campaign of preaching the coming of the Kingdom of Heaven. The Mass did not originate at the Last Supper. Jesus had laid an extensive groundwork for it. Along with his preaching and his miracles, Jesus also accepted invitations to dinners from everyone–from religious people like Simon the Pharisee (Lk 7:36-50) to outcasts like Levi the tax collector (Lk 5:27-32). He was invited for what he had to say–and probably also because he was a local celebrity. Some of his hosts disrespected him, and some were so open to him that they became disciples. In at least one instance, Jesus provided the meal–at the feeding of the five thousand.

Was that a Mass? The crowd had been with Jesus for three days listening to his preaching. They stayed though they had nothing to eat. At the end of the miraculous feeding, the crowd is ecstatic. They try to seize him and make him king, but he evades them. No, I guess it's not quite a Mass, because the spiritual understanding of Jesus' work is not yet present. The crowd would have made him an earthly ruler. And even though their understanding is on a par with that of the hierarchy for centuries until a few generations ago–religious leadership as political power–it is not sufficient.

All of these depictions of meals, together with the Eucharistic discourses in St. John's gospel if they reflect in any way the speech of the historical Jesus, are foreshadowings of the Mass. In the case of the Eucharistic discourses, if Jesus himself did not say these exact words, they at least represent the church's understanding of the Eucharist in the apostolic age. Jesus is himself the Bread of Life; the point of the Eucharist is not that we can touch the Lord, but that we through the Eucharist become ourselves the Bread of Life, the Word, the living incarnation of Jesus and his Father empowered to continue his work in the world.

Suppose someone should object that the imperative, "Do this in memory of me," was said only to the Twelve, the Apostolic College, the future bishops of the church. And that, therefore, no lay person should even think of celebrating the Mass in his or her own home.

Then we would have to discuss the Twelve. Who were they? The best Catholic scripture scholars believe that they were a group assembled by Jesus to represent the ingathering of the twelve tribes of Israel in the last days. They collectively symbolized Jesus' appeal to all Israel. In the view of these scholars, the Twelve were an unrepeatable event. As a group they had no successors. And, from all appearances, not many of them became leaders in the movement that Jesus left behind.

As for the apostles being bishops, the last apostle died before the idea of a monarchical bishop began to be suggested. Ignatius of Antioch, who was martyred ca. 107 CE, strongly favored the idea of the bishop, or overseer, as being the linchpin of every local church. Even so, he never mentions the bishop without also mentioning the presbyters (council of elders) and the deacons (religious ministers) of the church. In his speech, it almost seems as if these three church entities are on a par. So we must say that even with Ignatius, we do not yet see the arrival of the monarchical bishop who rules the church without recourse to others. It goes without saying that the priesthood has not yet emerged, except that Ignatius urges the bishops, where there are bishops,[16] to permit no one to offer the Eucharist whom the bishop has not authorized. Obviously, this is not what is happening during Ignatius's time. What he is urging is a power play by bishops. What is actually happening is the same practice depicted in the Acts of the Apostles.

In the Acts, when the Hellenists complain that their widows are being neglected in the daily distribution of food, what is the apostles' reply?

> "It is not right for us to neglect the word of God to serve at table. Brothers, select from among you seven reputable men, filled with the Spirit and wisdom, whom we shall appoint to this task, whereas we shall devote ourselves to prayer and to the ministry of the word." (Acts 6: 2-4)

The apostles are intent on devoting themselves "to prayer and to the ministry of the word." They don't mention the Eucharist, because the people are already celebrating the Eucharist themselves in their homes. This is apparent from an earlier passage of Acts:

> They (the Christian community) devoted themselves to the teaching of the apostles and to the communal life, to the breaking of the bread and to the prayers.... Every day they devoted themselves to meeting together in the temple area and to breaking bread in their homes. (Acts 2: 42,46)

The apostles go to the temple to pray and to teach the community, but the Christian community return to their homes to celebrate the Eucharist, "the breaking of the bread." Obviously, the apostles are not going round to each home to preside at this breaking of the

---

[16] There is no bishop at Rome at this time. Ignatius greets the bishop of each community first in each letter he sends. If, as at Rome, there is no bishop, no name appears.

bread. The people themselves, who hang on every word the apostles have to say, celebrate the Eucharist themselves at home.[17]

Example after example could be cited of churches founded by the apostle Paul and others, communities that then had to continue on their own after the departure of the apostle. From the glimpses of these communities provided by the New Testament, it is evident that there are no ordained ministers presiding over the liturgy. Such a development lies in the future. The Mass is in the hands of the people.

The Synagogue Service and the Mass

Scholars are agreed that the Mass took many of its earliest formative influences from the synagogue service at the time of the apostles. What was the synagogue? In the words of John L. McKenzie, S.J.,

> The synagogue was not, like the temple, a house where the deity dwelt, but a meeting house for prayer and the study of the law. It was a lay organization; sacrifice had no place in the synagogue cult, and if a priest happened to be present he was, except for certain courtesies, not distinguished from other members of the congregation. The government of the synagogue was committed to the elders of the synagogue, who were probably the elders of the community.[18]

No one held the office of presider at a synagogue service. Services were led by members of the congregation or by guests, both invited by the elders. Synagogues were among Jesus' favorite venues, and Paul and Barnabas, certainly, and other apostles, including Peter, probably, followed Jesus in speaking in synagogues. All were

---

[17] *The Mass*, Josef A. Jungmann, S.J., The Liturgical Press, 1976, pp 17-18; Jungmann believes that the surprising consistency, uniformity of practice, and realistic interpretation with which the church celebrates the Mass from the very beginning of its life may be due to Jesus' instructions after the resurrection, when he spoke to his followers about "the things that concern the reign of God" (Acts 1:3).

[18] *Dictionary of the Bible*, John L. McKenzie, S.J., Bruce, 1965; article: Synagogue, to whom I owe much of the following description.

familiar with the synagogue service, and so it is easy to see why, when the Mass became more of a public action, those who celebrated the Mass adopted freely from the synagogue service.

What was the synagogue service at the time of Christ? It began with the Shema (Dt 6:4-9), the Jewish profession of faith in the One God. This was followed by a long prayer improvised by one of the congregation. Next came readings from the law and the prophets in Hebrew and then translations or paraphrases of these passages into the current language–Aramaic for Jesus and the apostles. Then came a homily by a member of the congregation. To these services were added in time other prayers and the singing of psalms. If a priest were present, the priestly blessing was said to conclude the service ("The Lord bless you and keep you! The Lord let his face shine upon you...." Nb 6:24-26).

The synagogue began after the destruction of the Temple of Jerusalem in 587 BCE and the scattering of the Jews to foreign lands. Its persistence as a lay religious organization even after the rebuilding of the Temple is often credited with the survival of Judaism after the destruction of the Temple in 70 CE.

The *Didache* or Teaching of the Twelve Apostles

Scholars believe that this work (pronounced: did-ah-KAY or DID-ah-kay), from the Greek word for teaching) dates from the late first century or early second century.[19] It describes Christian church life as a world in which leadership roles are shifting from apostles, prophets, and teachers to bishops (overseers), presbyters (elders), and deacons (servants, helpers). The first three leaders tend to be itinerant and charismatic, while the second three are based in the community and are elected by the people.[20]

---

[19] *New Jerome Biblical Commentary* 80:42

[20] Paul provides one of the first descriptions of church order: "God has designated some people in the church to be: first apostles, second prophets, third teachers, then miracle workers, then healers, helpers, administrators, linguists." (1 Cor 12:28) Matthew has Jesus say, "Behold I send you prophets and wise men (teachers) and scribes..." probably reflecting the leadership of the Matthean community (Mt 23:34). Acts speaks of Paul and Barnabas as being among the prophets and teachers at Antioch in the early days of that church (AA 13:1).

The *Didache* is thought to be a composite work. It contains 16 chapters, the first six of which may derive from a pre-Christian manual for the instruction of Jewish converts. The rest of the work gives a vivid glimpse of the subapostolic Christian community and its approach to Baptism, fasting, the Eucharist, and the reception to be given to apostles and prophets (itinerant preachers, or missionaries) around the year 100 CE.

The fascinating thing to note about the *Didache* is that, after the first five or six chapters, which are addressed to "my child," the rest of the work is addressed to the Christian community at large, to the laity. There are emerging leadership roles, but as yet no clergy. The writer attempting to reproduce the teaching of the twelve apostles still presumes that the people baptize, celebrate the Eucharist, admit prophets and apostles and elect their leaders with a show of hands:

> Elect (Χειροτονήσατε), therefore, for yourselves bishops (overseers) and deacons (servants, helpers) worthy of the Lord, meek men, and not lovers of money, and truthful and approved, for they also minister to you the ministry of the prophets and teachers. Therefore do not despise them, for they are your honorable men together with the prophets and teachers. (Did XV:1-2)

The *Didache* has also preserved for us the very earliest example of a Eucharistic prayer, or anaphora. It bears a striking resemblance to the Jewish blessing, the *Birkat ha-Mazon*, or grace after meals, that scholars believe Jesus used at the Last Supper and that was to become a model for the Eucharistic prayers of the Christian church. I defer discussion of these two prayers, the Jewish and the Christian, to a fuller treatment later in this book.

Though there were references to the *Didache* in ancient times, the work itself was unknown to scholars and church historians until 1875 when it was discovered in the Patriarchal Library of Jerusalem at Constantinople. In this work, we today have an insight into the earliest years of the church, an insight that was unavailable to previous generations.

St. Justin Martyr

St. Justin, who was martyred in 165 CE, was one of those teachers of rhetoric and philosophy who were common in the ancient world. He, however, was a man of uncommon abilities. He gives us a view of the Mass in his time, and, through his writings, we begin to see the faint possibility of a hierarchy, though only the title, deacon, is mentioned. This is probably for the sake of secrecy in an age of persecutions. In his *First Apology*, addressed to the emperor Antoninus Pius, Justin describes Baptism and the Eucharist together, as the newly baptized person is permitted to join in the Mass of the community. The parts of the text that speak of the Mass are in boldface.

I will also relate the manner in which we dedicated ourselves to God when we had been made new through Christ; lest, if we omit this, we seem to be unfair in the explanation we are making. As many as are persuaded and believe that what we teach and say is true, and undertake to be able to live accordingly, are instructed to pray and to entreat God with fasting, for the remission of their sins that are past, we praying and fasting with them. Then they are brought by us where there is water and are regenerated in the same manner in which we ourselves were regenerated. For, in the name of God, the Father and Lord of the universe, and of our Savior Jesus Christ, and of the Holy Spirit, they then receive the washing with water.... (Chap. LXI)

But after we have thus washed him who has been convinced and has assented to our teaching, **we bring him to the place where those who are called brethren are assembled, in order that we may offer heartfelt prayers in common for ourselves and for the baptized [illuminated] person, and for all others in every place, that we may be counted worthy, now that we have** learned the truth, by our works also to be found good citizens and keepers of the commandments, so that we may be saved with an everlasting salvation. Having ended the prayers, we salute one another with a kiss. There is then brought to the president of the brethren bread and a cup of wine mixed with water; and he taking them, gives praise and glory to the Father of the universe, through the name of the Son and of the Holy Spirit, and offers thanks at considerable length for our being counted worthy to receive these things at His hands. And when he has concluded the prayers and thanksgivings, all the people present express their assent by saying Amen. This word Amen is the equivalent in the Hebrew language of γένοιτο [Greek: 'so be it']. And when the president has given thanks, and all the people have expressed their assent, those who are called by us deacons give to each of those present to partake of the bread and wine mixed with water over which the thanksgiving was pronounced, and to those who are absent they carry away a portion. (Chap. LXV)

And this food is called among us Εὐχαριστία [Eucharist], of which no one is allowed to partake but the one who believes that the things we teach are true, and who has been washed with the washing that is for the remission of sins, and unto regeneration, and who is so living as Christ has enjoined. For not as common bread and common drink do we receive these. But as Jesus Christ our Savior, having been made flesh by the Word of God, took both flesh and blood for our salvation, so also have we been taught that the food which is blessed by the prayer of His word, and from which our blood and flesh are nourished, by transmutation is the flesh and blood of that Jesus who was made flesh.

> **For the apostles, in the memoirs composed by them, which are called gospels, have thus delivered unto us what was enjoined upon them; that Jesus took bread, and when He had given thanks, said, "Do this in remembrance of Me; this is My body;" and that, after the same manner, having taken the cup and given thanks, He said, "This is My blood;" and gave it to them alone.... (Chap. LXVI)**

> **And on the day called Sunday, all who live in cities or in the country gather together in one place, and the memoirs of the apostles or the writings of the prophets are read, as long as time permits; then, when the reader has ceased, the president verbally instructs and exhorts to the imitation of these good things. Then we all rise together and pray, and, as we said before, when our prayer is ended, bread and wine and water are brought, and the president in like manner offers prayers and thanksgivings, according to his ability, and the people assent, saying Amen; and there is a distribution to each, and a participation in that over which thanks have been given, and to those who are absent a portion is sent by the deacons.... (Chap LXVII)**

In these passages, Justin gives two accounts of the Mass. In the first, he speaks of the Mass as being the privilege of those who have been baptized. He portrays the baptized person being brought to the (probably secret) place where "the brethren are assembled." Justin does not mention the service of the Word, but only the Eucharistic prayer and the communion (Chap. LXV). Then he speaks particularly about the institution narrative, the passage in the Mass containing the words, "This is my body...this is my blood," explaining how Jesus came to institute the Eucharist and telling why we do what we do (Chap. LXVI). We can probably infer from the importance assigned to these words that the words of the institution narrative were used in the Mass at that time.

Then Justin circles round and gives another brief summary of the Mass in which he indicates that the Service of the Word precedes the Canon, or Eucharistic prayer, and is a prominent part of the Mass (Chap. LXVII). In this chapter, he also lets us know that the celebrant of the Mass improvises the words of the Canon "according to his ability." The 'most important' part of the Mass is not yet a fixed formula.

Justin's writings do not yet give us any strong sense of a clerical hierarchy. He does not speak of the charismatic roles of prophets and teachers, however, who were prominent in New Testament descriptions of church order and in the *Didache*. By Justin's time, contemporary prophets seem to have disappeared. He speaks only of the ancient prophets. And, though he himself would qualify as a teacher, since he conducted his own school, and in Chapter LXI above he does use the words, "what we (Christians) teach and say"–thus probably including himself among the unofficial instructors of newcomers–nevertheless, as a teacher, he does not seem to function as an official leader of the church. His writings reflect the state of the church shortly before his death in 165 CE.

Hippolytus of Rome

Hippolytus is variously called in the tradition a saint, an antipope, a bishop, and a martyr. He probably was not a bishop but a presbyter and an opponent of several Roman bishops, Zephyrinus (198-217), Callistus (217-222), Urban (222-230), and Pontian (230-235). He was a conservative Christian pamphleteer, who took himself and his followers out of the church from around 217, when Callistus was elected, till shortly before his own death as a martyr along with the Roman bishop Pontian in the Sicilian mines (235). We are indebted to him for his depiction of the Catholic liturgy of his time and for showing us the beginnings of the hierarchy in the years preceding the year 235 CE. The work he left us was *The Apostolic Tradition*. He intended this small work as a protest against people who were not maintaining the traditions of the church as they had been handed down from the apostles. Hippolytus had no way of knowing that there were no bishops at the time of the apostles. But the document is remarkable in its similarity to some of the rites as we still observe them.

During Hippolytus's time the church was still subject to flare-ups of state persecutions followed by intermittent periods of peace. Masses were still conducted in Christians' homes or in the large halls rented or owned by professional teachers. The *ekklesía*, or church, was still the 'gathering' of Christians and not yet a church building. But it is obvious from the models that Christians are choosing from the Jewish scriptures that some at least (i.e., the incipient clergy) would like to have a full-blown priesthood and sanctuary as the Jews did before the time of Christ. The references below to the bishop as "high priest," "ministering as priests," and a "sanctuary" are, at this time, metaphors taken from the Jewish scriptures–metaphors on the verge of becoming cast-iron hierarchic usage, however. Those who would later be known as "priests" (Lat., sacerdotes, Gk., ιερεῖς; i.e., those who offer animal or other sacrifices) at this stage still go by the title "elders" (Lat., presbyteri; Gk., πρεσβύτεροι).[21]

Ordination, i.e., the "laying on of hands," was being used to set people up as bishops, presbyters, and deacons. Note, however, that Hippolytus's first sentence regarding the clergy is, "Let the bishop be ordained after he has been chosen (elected) by all the people." (ii.,1) The account then continues:

> And when he has been proposed and found acceptable to all, the people shall assemble on the Lord's day together with the presbyters (elders) and such bishops as may be present.
>
> With the agreement of all (the people) let the bishops lay hands on him and the presbyters stand by in silence.

---

[21] In the Latin translation of *The Apostolic Tradition* made in the late fourth or fifth century, however, in the section on the ordination of deacons, the word *sacerdotium* is used (signifying a priest who is not an *elder*, but one who offers *sacrifices*): "*[Diaconus] non sacerdotio ordinatur, sed in ministerio episcopi...*" "[The deacon] is not ordained to the priesthood, but to minister to the bishop..." This translation was made well after Constantine's Edict of Toleration of the Christians (313 A.D) and may reflect usage at that time, rather than the time when Hippolytus wrote.

And all shall keep silence praying in their heart for the descent of the Spirit.

After this, one of the bishops present at the request of all, laying his hand on him, shall pray thus, saying:

"O God and Father of our Lord Jesus Christ, Father of mercies and God of all comfort," "who dwell on high yet have respect unto the lowly," "who know all things before they come to pass;"

Who gave ordinances unto your church "by the Word of your grace;" who "foreordained from the beginning" the race of the righteous from Abraham, instituting princes and priests and leaving not your sanctuary without ministers; who from the foundation of the world have been pleased to be glorified in them whom you have chosen;

Now pour forth that Power which is from you, of "the princely Spirit" which you delivered to your beloved Child Jesus Christ, which he bestowed on your holy apostles who established the church which blesses you in every place to the endless glory and praise of your Name.

Father "who know the hearts (of all)" grant upon this your servant whom you have chosen for the episcopate to feed your holy flock and serve as your high priest, that he may unceasingly propitiate your countenance and offer to you the gifts of your holy church,

And that by the high priestly Spirit he may have authority "to forgive sins" according to your command, "to assign lots" according to your bidding, to "loose every bond" according to the authority you gave to the apostles, and that he may please you in meekness and a pure heart, "offering" to you "a sweet-smelling savor,"

Through your Child Jesus Christ our Lord, through whom to you be glory, might and praise, to the Father and to the Son with the Holy Spirit now and world without end. Amen.

This account then continues immediately with Hippolytus's depiction of the Eucharist, in a fashion similar to St. Justin's account of the Eucharist following a Baptism:

And when he has been made bishop let every one offer him the kiss of peace, saluting him, for he has been made worthy.

(Offertory) To him then let the deacons bring the oblation and he with all the presbyters laying his hand on the oblation shall say giving thanks:
The Lord be with you.
And the people shall say: And with your spirit.
Lift up your hearts.
We have them with the Lord.
Let us give thanks to the Lord.
(It is) meet and right.
And then he shall continue thus:

(Canon) We render thanks unto you, O God, through your beloved Child Jesus Christ, whom in the last times you sent to us as a savior and redeemer and angel of your counsel; Who is your Word inseparable (from you), through whom you made all things and in whom you were well-pleased; (Whom) you sent from heaven into the Virgin's womb and who, conceived within her, was made flesh and was shown to be your Son being born of the Holy Spirit and a Virgin; Who fulfilling your will and preparing for you a holy people stretched forth his hands for suffering that he might release from sufferings those who have believed in you; Who when he was betrayed to voluntary suffering that he might abolish death and rend the bonds of the devil and tread down hell and enlighten the righteous and establish the limit and demonstrate the resurrection: Taking bread (and) giving thanks to you he said: Take, eat: this is my body which is broken for you. Likewise also the cup, saying: This is my blood which is shed for you.

When you do this, you do my remembrance (anamnesis). Doing therefore the remembrance of his death and resurrection, we offer to you the bread and the cup, making Eucharist (or 'giving thanks') to you because you have made us worthy to stand before you and minister as priests to you. And we pray you that you would send your Holy Spirit upon the oblation of your holy church; grant to all your saints gathered together, who partake, that they may be filled with the Holy Spirit for the confirmation of their faith in truth. That we may praise and glorify you through your Child Jesus Christ through whom glory and honor be unto you with the Holy Spirit in your holy church now and world without end. Amen.[22]

For some reason, Hippolytus at this point discontinues his recitation of the Eucharistic celebration. He does not proceed to the Communion of the celebrant and the people. Possibly he was interested in describing the liturgy only insofar as it was distinctive for the new bishop. He, too, has omitted any mention of the Service of the Word. In fact, like Justin, he considers both of these elements of the Mass highly important and mentions them elsewhere in his text. And, it is worth repeating here, Hippolytus is not providing an exact text; he is in effect saying, the rite (ordination, Eucharist) should be conducted along these lines. The fact that he fails to mention the Service of the Word and the Communion are ample evidence of this.

Like Ignatius of Antioch, though, arguing in favor of the bishop as the 'first among equals,' (the others being the presbyters and the deacons) Hippolytus, too, is engaging in special pleading. He is arguing for a priestly ministry similar to that described in the Old Testament. He goes so far as to call the bishop the High Priest, the head of a priesthood in the same sense as the Jewish High Priest was the head of the Temple priesthood. The possibility of establishing a true hierarchy, though, will not occur until after

---

[22] Gregory Dix, *The Apostolic Tradition of St. Hippolytus of Rome* (London, S.P.C.K., 1937, reissued 1968) 2-9.

Constantine's edict of toleration of Christians in 313 CE. After that time, the church will be able to own property and build its own church buildings. The church isn't quite there yet, so long as the bishop has to call for the presbyters and the deacons to assemble together each day at an unnamed and therefore secret location which he, the bishop, shall appoint (xxxiii.1). And though Hippolytus refers fondly to a 'sanctuary,' presumably a temple-like building with an altar, the Christians of his time have no temple-like buildings and no altars.

It cannot be too highly emphasized that this witness provided by Hippolytus to the church's practice at the beginning of the third century was not available to scholars and church historians before the twentieth century. The Greek manuscripts of *The Apostolic Tradition* were lost almost immediately after the author's death. Though this pamphlet was written in Rome at the beginning of the third century, it did not have much currency there, probably because it seemed to be stating the obvious, depicting actual practice.

Over the following centuries, however, the *Apostolic Tradition* was translated into various languages at the eastern end of the empire, including Coptic, Arabic, and Ethiopic. It was adopted and expanded as part of a fourth century Greek work called the *Apostolic Constitutions*, and epitomized as well in that same work. Sometime in the fourth or fifth century, it returned to Rome as a translation into Latin made probably by a Greek-speaking Syrian. It was expanded and adapted in Greek, again in the fourth or fifth century and then that work was translated into Syriac in the seventh century as *The Testament of Our Lord*. Only the Syriac version survives. In modern times, a few fragments of the original Greek text have been found.

Only in 1916 did the Benedictine, Dom R.H. Connolly, argue in a scholarly monograph that all of these scattered documents in various languages had the lost work of Hippolytus, *The Apostolic Tradition*, as their source document. Thereafter, a small number of scholars set out to reconstruct the original document. Dom Gregory Dix published his reconstruction in 1937 and Dom Bernard Botte published his in 1963. These Benedictine scholars succeeded wonderfully. At least 95 percent of the original work has been recovered and the sense of the rest is easily discernible.

This small example of scholarly work on the recovery of Christian origins is but a single tile in a vast mosaic that has been progressively illuminating our understanding of the past for at least the last 150 years. It is the main reason why scholars today have a much better view of the origins of the Christian church than anyone has had since the time of the apostles.

A Summary: The Mass of the First Three Centuries

The way the Mass has been celebrated for most of our lives is not the way it was celebrated during the first years of the church. Then it was celebrated around a table, often by a family group. Early on it was part of a meal, not an ordinary meal, but a ritual meal modeled to a certain extent on the Paschal meal. Also at an early stage, the breaking of the bread and the drinking from the cup were brought together from the beginning and end of the meal, and certain elements of the synagogue service, like the scriptural readings and the singing of other psalms besides the *Hallel*,[23] were added. Because, for some early Christians, the meal distracted them from the object of the Mass–to remember and re-encounter the Lord–the early church soon dispensed with it.[24] The downside of this was that the ritual tended to distance the participants from reliving the occasion on which Jesus gave us this celebration and from reimagining Jesus in his human setting.

The earliest full liturgies for which we have written evidence, dating from the second through the fifth centuries, all included a service of the word and the Eucharistic prayer. The service of the word included readings and instruction, and the instruction was not limited to the presider, or presiders. "Psalms, hymns, and spiritual songs," in St. Paul's words,[25] were part of the entire rite. The Eucharistic prayer, or canon, is thought to have consisted of four parts: the thanksgiving[26], the institution

---

[23] The *Hallel* was a hymn comprised of Psalms 113-118 that the Jews recited on great feasts, notably on Passover.

[24] Cf. 1 Cor 11:17-34

[25] Col 3:16

[26] "In Hippolytus the items of this thanksgiving are four, for the action of the Word of God in Creation, in the Incarnation, in the Passion, at the Last Supper—in that order. It is important to note that of over sixty early liturgies,

narrative,[27] the remembrance of the Lord (anamnesis),[28] and an invocation on behalf of the community (sometimes called the epiclesis).[29] For myself, however, this may be making the Mass too technical for ordinary believers, who were, after all, its first celebrants. And I can imagine all of these four elements in a single prayer. Dismembering the Mass this way into "required elements" may well be like dismembering a chicken; when you have finished, the living is now dead.

It cannot be too strongly emphasized that, in the first three centuries, the entire Mass, including the Canon, was extemporized. It is probable that not even the institution narrative was pronounced according to a fixed formula. Only the broad elements of the Mass, and not the words themselves, were dictated by tradition.

---

one only, that of Sarapion, has not this arrangement," Gregory Dix, *The Apostolic Tradition*, p. xli. He notes, however, that the Roman Canon has undergone "dislocation." Hence, it retains only traces of this early arrangement.

[27] The institution narrative is the part of the Mass that begins, "On the night before he died" and contains the words, "This is my body...this is my blood."

[28] The anamnesis is the phrase "Do this in memory of me." It sometimes includes the prayers expanding the theme of our mindfulness of the Lord's command.

[29] *L'Ordinaire de la Messe, Texte Critique, Traduction et Études*, Bernard Botte, O.S.B. et Christine Mohrmann; Éditions du Cerf, Paris, 1953, p. 16.

"Do This in Memory of Me"
The Roman Mass and Roots of the Eucharistic Prayer

The Roman Mass

The Roman Mass, when it began to take form in the fourth and fifth centuries, probably included the following elements. The sung parts listed below in italics have been thought not to be originally Roman but early additions to the ritual that spread from Rome everywhere.

1. *Sung: The Entrance Song*
2. The Collect
3. The Epistle
4. *Sung: The Gradual and Alleluia*
5. The Blessing before the Gospel
6. The Gospel
7. The Homily
8. *Sung: The Offertory Song*
9. The Orate Fratres, the Secret, the Preface, Sanctus, Te Igitur and the rest of the Canon culminating in the Great Amen, the Lord's Prayer and the prayer immediately following, and the kiss of peace
10. *Sung: The Communion Song*
11. The Communion
12. The Postcommunion
13. The Ite Missa Est.[30]

Not included in the early Roman Mass were a number of foreign elements, Greek and French, that made their appearance in the Roman Mass at various times from the fifth century to the later

---

[30] *Liturgica Historica*, Edmund Bishop, Oxford University Press, 1918, p. 7. I owe almost all of the breakdown of the Roman and non-Roman elements of the Mass to this source.

middle ages. These elements were part of the Mass as it was celebrated by Western Catholicism until the Second Vatican Council. In fact, some of them remain still:

1. The Asperges (You will sprinkle), the psalm Iudica me (Judge me), and everything said by the priest as he ascended the altar
2. The Kyrie eleison (Lord, have mercy) is much earlier, 2nd half of the 5th century; adopted from the East.
3. The Gloria in excelsis and the Creed were introduced in the 6th and 11th centuries, respectively.
4. All of the prayers accompanying the acts of the Offertory and the censing of the altar, the Lavabo ("I will wash my hands), and the Suscipe Sancta Trinitas ("Accept, O Holy Trinity) are late medieval (French).
5. The Sanctus (Holy, Holy, Holy), from the Greek, was probably not being used in Rome before the 5th century.
6. It is not certain whether the Agnus Dei (Lamb of God) was in use in Rome before the 7th century.
7. The three prayers said before the communion ("Lord Jesus Christ, who said to your apostles...", "Lord Jesus Christ, son of the living God,...", "May the reception of your body, O Lord Jesus Christ...") and all that follows the postcommunion except the Ite Missa est are all late & borrowed.[31]

In other words, though the Roman Mass was a fairly spare ritual in the fourth century, the clergy began making additions of words and entire prayers to the Mass early on and continued doing so over the centuries. The following is a partial comparison of the Canon as reported by St. Ambrose in the late fourth century and the Canon of the Council of Trent:

Ambrose	The Roman Canon
Make this offering on our behalf creditable, spiritual, acceptable, because it is the embodiment of the body and blood of our lord Jesus Christ.	And this offering, O God, do you in all ways please deem blessed, creditable, ratified, spiritual, acceptable, that it may become for us the body and blood of your most

---

[31] Ibid.

beloved son, our lord Jesus Christ.

Who the day before he suffered took bread in his holy hands, looked up to heaven to you, holy father almighty eternal God, giving thanks he blessed it, broke it, and handed over the broken-off pieces to his apostles and disciples saying:

Who the day before he suffered, took bread in his holy and venerable hands and, with his eyes lifted up to heaven, to you God, his Father almighty, giving thanks to you, he blessed it, broke it, and gave it to his disciples, saying:

Take all of you and eat of this; for this is my body that will be broken in pieces for many.
Likewise also the chalice after dinner, the day before he suffered, he took it, looked up to heaven to you, holy father almighty eternal God; giving thanks he blessed it and handed it over to his apostles and disciples saying:
Take and drink of this all of you; for this is my blood.

Take and eat of this all of you. For this is my body.

In a similar way after dinner, taking also this splendid chalice in his holy and venerable hands, again giving thanks to you, he blessed it and gave it to his disciples, saying:

Take and drink from it all of you. For this is the chalice of my blood, the blood of the new and eternal testament–the mystery of faith–which will be poured out for you for the forgiveness of sins.

Every time you do this you will be commemorating me until I come again.

Every time you do this, you will be remembering me.

And so, remembering his most glorious passion and resurrection from death and ascension into heaven, we offer to you this spotless victim, this holy bread and chalice of eternal life,

For this reason also, we, your servants, O Lord, and also your holy people, remembering Christ your son, our Lord, his blessed passion, as well as his resurrection from death, and also his glorious ascension into the heavens, do offer to your splendid majesty from your gifts and presents a pure victim, a holy victim, a spotless victim, the holy bread of eternal life and the chalice of perpetual salvation.

and we ask and pray that you will lift up this offering to your altar on high by the hands of your holy

May you see fit to look upon it with a kindly and serene countenance and hold it acceptable, as you saw fit to angels,

hold acceptable the gifts of your child, Abel the just, and the sacrifice of our patriarch, Abraham, and what your high priest, Melchisedech, offered to you–a holy sacrifice, a spotless victim.

as you saw fit to accept the gifts of your child, Abel the just, and the sacrifice of our patriarch, Abraham, and what your high priest, Melchisedech offered to you.

Humbly we ask you almighty God, command these offerings to be carried all the way to your altar on high by the hands of your holy angel in the sight of your divine majesty, so that as many of us as take the body and blood of your son from the sharing of this altar may be filled with every heavenly blessing and grace.

32

33

The similarities between the Canon of the fourth century and that of the sixteenth century are unmistakable. So is the added verbiage. In the Latin it is the difference between 179 words for Ambrose's Canon and 256 words for the Canon of Trent. The additions amount to a 43 percent increase. On the other hand, even Ambrose's Canon shows the effect of calcification, of rote memory. He repeats "the day before he suffered took (bread, the cup) in his holy hands, looked up to heaven to you, holy father almighty eternal God, giving thanks he blessed it, ... and handed over...". The Roman Canon avoids this rote repetition, though by the time of Trent it had stuffed many more words and theological ideas into the sausage-casing.

The editorial reforms to the text of the Mass following Vatican II went a long way toward cutting out repetitious language and making the Mass text more the expression of a faith community, rather than a largely clerical ritual. It only remains to put the Mass back into the hands of the community.

Let us, by all means be simple and remember the Lord's words: "In praying do not babble on endlessly like the pagans, who

---

[32] *Des Sacrements, Des Mystères*; ed., tr. & annot. by Dom Bernard Botte, O.S.B.; Éditions du Cerf; Paris; 1949; V,21,22,VI,26,27; my translation from the Latin

[33] *Missale Romanum*; Desclée & Socii; 1951; my translation

think that they will be heard because of their many words," and "Let your 'yes' be 'yes' and your 'no' be 'no.'"[34] For, as he says in the same place, Your Father knows what you need before you ask him.

The Ancient Origins of the Eucharistic Prayer

Now is the time to look at the deepest roots of the Eucharistic prayer. Cesare Giraudo's 1989 study of the literary structure of the Eucharistic prayer[35] traces its literary form back to the second millennium BCE. Not that the content of our Eucharistic prayer originated in that remote age, but in fact the literary form that it follows owes a great deal to the first utterances of the covenant, or alliance, between God and his people. These in turn were adapted from ancient near-Eastern treaties of vassalage between kings and powerful families who supported them. In exchange for offering their service to the king, the family received a deed of land, which they were to hold in perpetuity, so long as they continued to render their service.

This exchange of land for service describes the covenant relationship between the God of Israel and his people. And the literary form in which it is expressed can be followed with remarkable consistency through the literature of the Old Testament, into Jewish domestic and synagogue liturgy, and into the earliest Eucharistic prayers. And, surprisingly, many, many forms of Eucharistic prayers are recorded from the Mediterranean world in the first ages of the church.

In essence, this literary form has two parts. The first part is a remembrance of the Covenant, the alliance between God and his people, and of all the good things that God has done for us throughout our history, despite our backsliding, despite our failures to live up to his gracious gift to us. The second part was often preceded by one or more Hebrew particles, which were carried over into Greek, and are translated, "And now," or "Now, therefore," or simply "Therefore." The second part of this literary form called upon God to come to the aid of his people, to uphold

---

[34] Mt 6:7; 5:37

[35] Cesare Giraudo, *La Struttura Letteraria della Preghiera Eucharistica* (Rome: Editrice Pontificio Istituto Biblico, 1989).

his part of the alliance, and in the Eucharistic prayers to send down his Spirit upon us and upon our offerings.

Earlier, we said that most scholars believe that Jesus used the Jewish blessing after meals as the first Eucharistic prayer and that that form shaped the earliest Christian Eucharistic prayers.

What Eucharistic Prayer Did Jesus Use?

The *Birkat ha-Mazon*, or Blessing After Meals, was part of the Jews' domestic liturgy during Jesus' lifetime. So this was a prayer used at home, not in the synagogue. The gospels, in telling us about the Last Supper, do not give us the text of this prayer. They take that for granted. Instead what they give us is a description of what Jesus was doing, his own interpretation of his actions, and his instructions to us to continue the practice in his memory.

Through a tumbling cascade of ironies of religious history, the Jews and the early Christians grew apart from one another and became enemies; Jewish Christianity eventually died out in favor of Gentile Christianity; the early Christians, most of whom came from the lower classes of Mediterranean civilization, were subject to persecutions, which interfered with their ability to understand and maintain their own traditions, while Jewish oral traditions, which did not begin to be written down till around 200 CE, underwent inevitable changes under the influences of the Jews' own historical experience.

As a result, the earliest written examples of the *Birkat ha-Mazon* date from the ninth and tenth centuries, while the earliest written examples of the anaphora, the Eucharistic prayer, date from the turn of the first century. You would think it would be like comparing apples and oranges to try to match these two prayers. But we have two advantages. One is the remarkable stability of the Jews' oral tradition. The other is the wisdom that scholars have developed in dealing with early texts.

The *Birkat ha-Mazon* consisted originally of three prayers: One blessing God for the world and all that is in it; one thanking him for the land of Israel; and one asking God to watch over the Jewish people, the city of Jerusalem, and the Temple and to restore the kingdom of David. Now it is a fairly safe rule with prayers that they tend to grow in size through additions and refinements over the passage of time. And so, other things being equal, the shorter text tends to be the earlier text.

Here is one of the shortest texts of the *Birkat ha-Mazon* to come down to us. It is that of the Rabbi, Saadja Gaon. It dates from the tenth century:

> Blessed are you, Lord our God, king of the world,
> nourishing us and the whole world with goodness,
> grace, kindness, and mercy;
> > Blessed are you, Lord, nourishing the world.

> We will give thanks to you, Lord our God,
> for you gave us as an inheritance
> a land, desirable, good, and wide,
> a covenant and a law,
> life and food.
> And for all these things we give you thanks
> and we bless your name for ever and ever.
> > Blessed are you, Lord, for the land and for food.

> Have mercy on us, Lord our God,
> on Israel, your people,
> and on Jerusalem, your city, your sanctuary, and your dwelling-place,
> and on Sion, the seat of your glory,
> and on the great and holy house upon which your name is invoked.
> And restore the reign of your servant David to its place in our time,
> and quickly build Jerusalem.[36]

This prayer looks as if it could well have been said during the lifetime of Jesus, except for the very last clause, "and quickly build Jerusalem." That clause looks like a later addition, for two reasons. First, God's care has already been asked for Jerusalem earlier in that same section of the prayer. So this later mention

---

[36] Anton Hänggi-Irmgard Pahl, *Prex Eucharistica* (Freiburg, Universitätsverlag Freiburg Schweiz, 3rd edn, 1998), 10f., from their Latin version of the Hebrew

seems redundant. Second, the earlier mention of Jerusalem assumes that the city is intact as God's sanctuary and dwelling-place, while this later mention assumes it needs rebuilding.

Now the Romans sacked Jerusalem and destroyed the Temple in 70 CE. They laid Jerusalem completely waste in 135 CE. So the last clause would seem to have been added sometime after 70 CE at the earliest.

There is also some question whether this prayer would have been said by Jesus in exactly this manner. While the prayer expresses concerns that were definitely on the minds of many Jews during the first century, Jesus, being a Galilean prophet, looked on Jerusalem as the provisional capital of his religion, not the permanent one. He said to the Samaritan woman, "The hour is coming when neither on this mountain (Mt. Gerizim in Samaria, where the Samaritans worshiped) nor in Jerusalem will you worship the Father.... but the hour is coming, and is now here, when true worshipers will worship the Father in Spirit and truth." (Jn 4:21-24) Obviously he did not fully support the Temple and its practices, as the incident of the "cleansing of the Temple" showed.

But he loved the Jewish people, as his lament over Jerusalem conveys: "Jerusalem, Jerusalem,...how many times would I have gathered your children together under my wings as a hen gathers her chicks; but you would not." (Mt 23:37)

And so when we read that the two disciples on the road to Emmaus finally recognize Jesus "in the breaking of the bread"–that is, in his Eucharistic action–it is likely that Jesus changed this prayer to reflect what he intended by the Eucharist. The mere breaking of bread would not suffice to convey his ideas. The only remaining elements in "the breaking of the bread" are the prayer itself and what else he said besides the prayer.

We can gain some idea of what Jesus may have changed in the prayer by considering the earliest Eucharistic prayer to emerge into the light of history at around 100 CE. By looking at that prayer, which is found in the *Didache*, or *Teaching of the Twelve Apostles*, and comparing it with the earliest likely version of the Jewish *Birkat-ha-Mazon*, we can make some educated guesses as to what changes in the prayer may have seemed to his disciples uniquely characteristic of Jesus. Here are the two prayers side-by-side:

The *Birkat ha-Mazon* according to Rabbi Saadja Gaon (10th cent. CE)

Blessed are you, Lord our God, king of the world,
nourishing us and the whole world with goodness, grace, kindness, and mercy;
Blessed are you, Lord, nourishing the world.

We will give thanks to you, Lord our God,
for you gave us as an inheritance
a land, desirable, good, and wide,
a covenant and a law,
life and food.
And for all these things we give you thanks
and we bless your name for ever and ever.
Blessed are you, Lord, for the land and for food.

Have mercy on us, Lord our God,
on Israel, your people,
and on Jerusalem, your city,

The Christian *Birkat ha-Mazon*, according to the *Didache*, X, 2-5 (ca. 100 CE)[37]

We give you thanks, holy Father,
because of your holy name
which you have made to dwell in our hearts,
and because of the knowledge and faith and immortality
which you have made known to us through Jesus, your child.
To you be glory forever!

You, almighty Lord,
created all things because of your name;
food and drink you gave to human beings for their enjoyment,
that they might give thanks to you.
But to us you have freely given spiritual food and drink
for eternal life through Jesus, your child.
For all these things, we give you thanks,
for you are mighty.
To you be glory forever!

Remember, Lord, your church;
remove it from all evil
and perfect it in your love,
and gather it from the four

---

[37] From Giraudo's Latin, p. 250, with an eye to the Greek in *The Apostolic Fathers*, ed. & trans. by Kirsopp Lake, Harvard Univ. Press-William Heinemann, Ltd., 1912; pp. 322, 324

your sanctuary, and your
dwelling-place,
and on Sion, the seat of your
glory,
and on the great and holy house
upon which your name is
invoked.
And restore the reign of your
servant David to its place in
our time.

winds, sanctified,
into your kingdom, which you
have prepared for it.
For yours is the power and the
glory forever! Amen.

The first thing to notice is the rough structural equivalence of the two series of prayers. The second thing is that both the Jewish and the Christian prayer follow the structure outlined by Cesare Giraudo. The first two sections recite the good things that God has done for his people; the third section calls upon him to watch over his people.

In the first pair of prayers, God who nourishes the whole world with goodness, grace, kindness, and mercy in the Jewish prayer is compared with God who dwells in our hearts thanks to the knowledge and faith and immortality made known to us by Jesus Christ.

In the second pair of prayers, God is thanked for the land, the covenant, the law, and for life and food, in the Jewish prayer, and in the Christian prayer for food and drink and the ability to enjoy them; but also for spiritual food and drink, and for eternal life, through Jesus, the Child of God.

The final set of prayers asks God's care and concern for the people of Israel, for Jerusalem, for the Temple, and for the restoration of the reign of David. The church, the messianic gathering, stands in the same place as the people of Israel in the last Christian prayer, which asks for the church's removal from all evil and for perfection in the love of God. The messianic kingdom of David is replaced by the messianic kingdom of Jesus Christ. And the Temple is not mentioned in the Christian version.

What light does this comparison shed on the Eucharistic prayer of Jesus? Perhaps the best way to answer that question would be to recast the *Birkat ha-Mazon* in the light of the first-century Christian prayer, and so arrive at something that Jesus might have said in his own time.

> We give you thanks, Father,
> because of your holy name
> and for the spirit of wisdom and understanding
> that you have poured into our hearts,
> and for nourishing us
> with the knowledge of your kingdom
> and your loving kindness.

> We give you thanks, Father,
> because, by your word, you created all things;
> food and drink for human beings to enjoy,
> and heavenly food and drink
> for eternal life through the Son of Man.
> For all these things, we give you thanks.

> Remember, Father,
> those whom you have called together
> in the name of your Son;
> keep us from evil,
> perfect us in your love,
> and let us see the coming of your kingdom
> in our own time.
> Amen.

If after this short prayer, or something like it, the unknown personage in the inn on the road to Emmaus then broke the bread and said, "Take and eat. This is my body, which was broken for you," it is no wonder the disciples' eyes were opened to the presence of Jesus who was dead and was now risen.

The point of this exercise is to describe how brief the Eucharist was at its beginning and to suggest the irreducible minimum for a Mass prayer. Remember the long talk that the two disciples had with Jesus along the road. That took the place of the service of the word in the Mass. After that, while they were in the presence of Jesus in their hearts and minds, it only remained to break the bread and eat it and to drink from the cup which were and are his body and blood.

A Bare-Bones Mass

What is the Mass, then, reduced to its essentials? As in my experience with Ed Tryba in that house-church in 1967, it is a prayerful, scriptural remembrance of Jesus Christ and a 'breaking of bread' in his memory; it is a sharing of the Body of Christ that makes us the Body of Christ, the church.

Our celebration of the Mass has four characteristics:

- a deep, prayerful, scriptural reflection that revives in our memories the life of the Lord and, more broadly, the experience of God's dealings with his people
- a thanksgiving to God the Father for all of his gifts, especially for Jesus' life and work on earth and his continued presence among us in the Holy Spirit,
- an urgent prayer that God will save us and all of his people, and finally,
- "the breaking of the bread;" our sharing of table fellowship with the Lord and in his memory, as he asked us to do.

This is all done in a spirit of prayer–of adoration, thanksgiving, and joy for the wonderful gift of Jesus' presence that we have been given. The Mass is an expression of unity, or solidarity, with our brothers and sisters now present and with the rest of the church throughout time. And the joy is communal, a sharing with our fellow believers. If, on the other hand, we feel great sadness and need, we should bring all of that before the Lord. He is our great Consoler.

The period just after Mass can well be an occasion for a light meal and conversation.

Our offerings count as well. In the second century, according to St. Justin, it had become a custom for the faithful to bring to the Sunday gathering of the community gifts produced by their life and work. They were brought for the relief of the poor and the carrying out of good works in Jesus' name. These were accepted by the leadership of the community and used for the charitable purposes for which they were brought forward. Although such offerings are not an essential part of the Mass, they are an essential part of the following of Christ. And, in the absence of a leadership we can trust, we should carry out these charitable works on our own, joining with other members of our community as occasion presents itself.

With its deepest roots in Jesus Christ, ours is a revolutionary faith. In the first three centuries of our religion, before we had churches and altars, when the idea of a hierarchy was just a gleam in an emerging bishop's eye, the masses of lay people who made up the church carried out what Hans Küng calls "a gentle revolution."[38] Individual church members overcame the Roman Empire by their generosity to others, the simplicity of their motives, and the solidarity of all of the faithful with one another regardless of wealth or class barriers or race or sex. All shared the same Eucharist, carried out the same acts of charity to others, ministered to one another's needs, and endured the same persecutions. It is ironic that the church with its gentleness conquered the Roman Empire before Constantine's Edict of Toleration in 313 CE, only to be conquered in turn by Rome's imperialistic spirit after receiving its earthly freedom.

It is important that we turn away decidedly from Roman imperialism wherever it may appear, certainly in our leadership structures, but in the Mass as well. Jesus was a revolutionary, but the revolutionary who washed the feet of his disciples was not an imperialist, not an authoritarian.

Practical First Steps to Celebrating Mass

This chapter should have given you a sense of the Mass as it was when Jesus gave it to us. I have made every effort to show how the Mass was celebrated by the earliest Christians and how it expanded and changed as it moved from the Jewish culture of Jesus' time into the Greek culture and especially into the culture of imperial Rome.

Reduced to its bare essentials, the Mass can be very brief. Some references to the Mass in the New Testament, however, portray it as the final action culminating an often long session of

---

[38] *The Catholic church: A Short History*, Hans Küng, tr. John Bowden, Modern Library, 2001, p. 30.

teaching or preaching about Jesus and his place in the history of God's dealings with his people. In the Acts of the Apostles, St. Luke gives us what appears to be his first-person account of Paul, who had just arrived in Troas (Acts 20:7-12):

> On the first day of the week when we gathered to break bread, Paul spoke to them because he was going to leave on the next day, and he kept on speaking until midnight. There were many lamps in the upstairs room where we were gathered, and a young man named Eutychus who was sitting on the window sill was sinking into a deep sleep as Paul talked on and on. Once overcome by sleep, he fell down from the third story and when he was picked up, he was dead.
>
> Paul went down, threw himself upon him, and said as he embraced him, "Don't be alarmed; there is life in him." Then he returned upstairs, broke the bread, and ate; after a long conversation that lasted until daybreak, he departed. And they took the boy away alive and were immeasurably comforted.

Once again, as we have pointed out earlier, "the breaking of the bread" is the New Testament's way of referring to Jesus' characteristic action in celebrating Mass–after the service of the word. In this case, St. Paul must have spoken for at least eight hours. And the Eucharistic portion of this Mass came briefly in the middle of the night.

The Mass can be long or short. The important thing is that it succeed in focusing our minds and hearts powerfully on God the Father and on Jesus with the help of his Holy Spirit.

Approach and Attitude

You and I, through our contributions to the Roman Catholic church as lay people over the past decades and centuries, ought to be entitled to the full use of all of our church's assets. That may be expecting too much, however, from this hierarchy. And we do not wish to compromise the priests, who are our natural allies, or alienate them unduly from their taskmasters in the hierarchy. I would recommend using the texts of the Mass developed after Vatican II with whatever changes you may think necessary for the sake of inclusive language or with adaptations based on the history of the Mass given above. This is one way of providing a bridge for future reconciliation with these "separated brethren" in the hierarchy.

Study the Mass texts with a view to extemporaneous adaptations of the parts of the Mass based on a thorough understanding of what they mean to convey.

Follow the cycle of readings (A, B, and C) as prescribed by the current liturgical leadership. Just make sure the sense of the scripture is maintained. I would advise against substituting non-scriptural readings for the scripture readings of the Mass. That would be likely to change the very nature of the Mass.

If you choose to have one main celebrant rather than several, rotate the role of presider among several men and women.

Don't limit the membership of your 'house church' to the same people or even the location to the same house. Invite new people as often as possible. This prevents the group from going stale. Do not invite people who would be scandalized by what we are doing. Make sure they have a proper understanding of the Lay Catholic Renewal movement. The Catholic church is our church in the fullest sense of those words–its most important ritual observance, the Mass, began among the laity. It is our birthright as followers of Jesus Christ. We are simply bringing it back home.

Keep attending Sunday Mass at your parish. Do not substitute a home Mass for your Sunday observance. We wish to maintain the unity of the church, not destroy it. A monthly home Mass should serve as a shot in the arm to your faith and a chance to exchange faith experiences with fellow Catholics. There are a lot of disgruntled Catholics out there. Some have stopped going to Mass entirely because of the misconduct of our church's self-appointed leadership and the inhospitable environment our 'leaders' have created in the church. We have to assure these disaffected Catholics that Jesus Christ is in control. He has not left us orphans.

The current leadership have thoroughly discredited themselves, but they are still Catholics. We must continue to hope that they will come to a proper understanding of leadership in the church. They cannot continue to act in defiance of the Holy Spirit as evidenced among the laity. And, until they eliminate the notion of hierarchy, we must leave the door open for them.

But actual control of the church has already been taken away from them. As few as we are and as seemingly powerless, the Lord has seen fit to give us the kingdom. We will make mistakes, but I hope they will not be mistakes of arrogant authoritarianism. Our hearts and minds are in the right place. We should not let our dispute with the hierarchy become a cause for division–or for a division greater than the one the hierarchy have already created in the church between themselves and the laity.

Our dispute with the hierarchy is over governance, over who controls the church. The hierarchy believe that they are in control. We say, No, Jesus Christ is the head of the church, and he governs it mildly through his Holy Spirit. How he accomplishes this is the subject of the next chapter.

Governance in the Church

> "You know that the rulers of the Gentiles lord it over them, and the great ones make their authority over them felt. But it shall not be so among you. Rather, whoever wishes to be great among you shall be your servant; whoever wishes to be first among you shall be your slave...." [Mt 20:25-27]

> "Who, then, is the faithful and prudent servant, whom the master has put in charge of his household to distribute to them their food at the proper time?.... But if that wicked servant says to himself, 'My master is long delayed,' and begins to beat his fellow servants,...the servant's master will come on an unexpected day and at an unknown hour and will punish him severely...." [Mt 24:45-51]

These two quotations from the New Testament give some idea of the extent and the limits of governance in the church that Jesus Christ founded. Christ is the leader. Christ is the master. He leads those who love him. His servants carry out affirmative duties toward his flock. And just as he himself never punished anyone during his earthly life, so his servants have no business punishing people on earth for their supposed shortcomings. His servants are in the business of helping. They are in the business of serving others, building them up, not tearing them down.

The Catholic church has gone far astray in this matter. Not only has it beaten other human beings, including the servants of the Master, it has deprived them of their homes and livelihoods, tortured them, murdered them, and instructed the rulers of 'Christian' governments to do the same. It launched and encouraged the launching of horrendous wars, of which the Crusades, which included the sack and despoliation of the Christian city of Constantinople, are run-of-the-mill examples. It has denied people of its own faith and other faiths the freedom of their consciences, depriving them of their physical freedom, life, and property because of what they believed. For more than a century, during the Albigensian Crusade, it persecuted and slaughtered the Cathars for trying to lead lives more centered on the gospel and for disagreeing with the Roman hierarchy. Best known to us who are so enamored of science, it persecuted and imprisoned Galileo for his scientific findings and, incidentally, for being a better theologian than his inquisitor, Cardinal Robert Bellarmine. For his devotion to the institutional church, Bellarmine was later canonized as a saint by the hierarchy.

And yet today this same Official Catholic Church, the weapons only recently wrenched from its hands by secular governments, continues to rob all the theologians it can still lay hands on of the freedom of their consciences. In practical terms, this means that priests and men and women religious fall chiefly within the hierarchy's villainous grasp. Lay people, unless they happen to be Catholic theologians teaching at a Catholic college or university, escape notice.

The list of Catholic scholars who have been savaged personally and professionally by the Vatican campaign of thought control is probably a long one. I must say 'probably' because the Vatican acts in secret in these matters. Only in unusual cases does the name of the scholar "under investigation" become public. A very short list of respected theologians recently persecuted by the Vatican in a process that allows the victim no rights and no recourse would include the names of Hans Küng, Leonardo Boff, and Gustavo Gutiérrez.[39]

Küng, one of the most important *periti* (experts) at Vatican II, first came under Vatican scrutiny in 1967 for his book, *The Church*. Scrutiny intensified for his books, *Infallible? An Inquiry* (1970), questioning papal infallibility, and *On Being a Christian* (1974). In 1979, his commission to teach Catholic theology was revoked by the Vatican. Because his scholarship is respected by his peers in the academic world, he managed to continue teaching and writing in a post not under the control of the Vatican.

Leonardo Boff, a Franciscan, and Gustavo Gutiérrez, now a Dominican, were attacked during the 1980s in the Vatican's largely successful effort to destroy liberation theology in Latin America. The name of the movement came from Gutiérrez's 1971 book, *A Theology of Liberation*, which the Vatican considered to be a Marxist view of the gospel. In 1983, the Vatican pressured the

---

[39] The whole story of Küng, Boff, and Gutiérrez is told in the book, *Cardinal Ratzinger: The Vatican's Enforcer of the Faith*, by John L. Allen, Jr.; Continuum; NY; 2000.

Peruvian bishops to condemn Gutiérrez, and they might have done so but for a stirring endorsement of the orthodoxy of Gutiérrez's theology sent to the bishops by Karl Rahner, probably the greatest Catholic theologian of the twentieth century. It came scarcely two weeks before Rahner's death in 1984.

Boff was not as fortunate, probably because he comes from Brazil, the largest Catholic country in the world, and one where the Vatican wished to make an example. Summoned to Rome that same year, 1984, for an examination of his book, *Church: Charism and Power*, he was accompanied by three Brazilian bishops who supported him. When there was no mention of censure at the end of the meeting, the Brazilians thought they had won their case. Not so. Boff was silenced in 1985, with the silencing lifted in 1986. The Vatican then blocked publication of a book in 1987. In the years following, he was repeatedly asked to clarify or modify his views. In 1991, he was asked to stop editing the Franciscan publication, *Vozes*, and in 1992 he was banned from teaching and subjected to preventive censorship. That was the last straw. He announced he was leaving the priesthood. He continues to lecture and to write.

Playing devil's advocate we can ask, 'Doesn't the church (i.e., the hierarchy) have a right to control the way church theology is taught?' There is only one answer to that question, because if you answer 'Yes,' you justify the crucifixion of Jesus Christ.

The High Priests, too, thought that they had a right to stifle an embarrassing prophetic voice. They didn't have that right, and neither does the current High Priesthood. We Catholics have to learn that we, the church, are a flock, not a police-state exercising thought control through its 'magisterium' or a corporation with an inflexible corporate line of thinking. At best, we bleat. Our thoughts are puny compared to God's. But God makes sense out of our cacophony. We must put our trust in the Lord and not in human beings. Human beings are no substitute for the Lord God, who lives in us in the Holy Spirit sent by God's son, Jesus Christ. The Vatican is trying very hard to substitute itself for that Trinity. Nevertheless, the "magisterium" (teaching function) belongs to

Jesus Christ alone. He is the sole Master.[40] Jesus' teaching office, or magisterium, does not belong by right or by appointment to any human being. It is a prophetic function. Prophets are chosen by God. They will always be critical of an institutional church for the same reasons they are critical of the world: both are human creations with significant flaws. At best, we who are believers can only share in Christ's teaching action when he chooses us for the task.

The Example of St. Peter

Why did St. Matthew, when he came to write his gospel, focus such attention on St. Peter that later generations of hierarchical leaders appealed to him as their prototype?

Matthew is the only one of the four evangelists who records Jesus as saying,

> "Blessed are you, Simon son of Jonah. For flesh and blood has not revealed this to you, but my heavenly Father. And so I say to you, you are Peter, and upon this rock I will build my church, and the gates of the netherworld shall not prevail against it.
>
> "I will give you the keys to the kingdom of heaven. Whatever you bind on earth shall be bound in heaven; and whatever you loose on earth shall be loosed in heaven." (Mt 16:17-19)

What was Matthew doing? In fact, he was resurrecting Peter from the dustbin of church history.

Peter had been Jesus' number two man, a natural leader, the spokesman for the Twelve while Jesus was alive. He is portrayed as headstrong, impulsive, even boastful. "Though all may have their faith in you shaken, mine will never be".... "Even though I should have to die with you, I will not deny you." (Mt 26:33,35) But in the crisis of Jesus' arrest he failed. He made a supreme mistake. He denied Christ. Afterward, seeing what he had done, he went out and wept bitterly.

---

[40] Cf. Mt 23:8-10 "You have one teacher and you are all brothers and sisters.... Do not be called 'Master'[i.e., teacher]; you have but one master, the Messiah."

Some of the stories of the resurrection suggest that Peter was the first witness of the risen Christ. (Lk 24:34; 1 Co 15:5) In the first part of the Acts of the Apostles, chapters 1-12, Peter is the leader of the Christian community at Jerusalem. He seems fully rehabilitated. But after chapter 12, he largely disappears from Acts, and James the brother of the Lord becomes leader at Jerusalem. Peter evidently went to Antioch, which was where the church was opening its membership to the Gentiles. At Antioch, Peter and Paul come into conflict over the question of eating with the Gentiles (Gal 2:11-14). Peter is intimidated by emissaries from James. Later, in the Acts of the Apostles, when the mission of Paul and Barnabas to the Gentiles is questioned by "some who had come down from Judea" (Jerusalem), it was decided to put this question to the apostles and elders in Jerusalem. Peter speaks in favor of the mission to the Gentiles, but it is James, the Lord's brother, who renders the decision.[41] Clearly, Peter is a figure of great authority, but he is not seen as the head of the universal church, not even by the Twelve.

It is possible that Peter may have ceded the leadership of the Jerusalem church to James in order to embark on a mission to the Gentiles, similar to that of Paul.[42] Some of the Corinthians call themselves the party of Cephas, i.e., Peter. (1 Co 1:12; 3:22) And the First Letter of Peter, though probably not written by him, claims to have been written from Babylon, a frequent code-name for Rome, suggesting that he may have reached that city in his travels. Then there is the tradition recorded in 1 Clement 5 that Peter, indeed, died in Rome in the same persecution as Paul, probably that of Nero ca. 64 CE, both of them "because of unrighteous zeal (or jealousy)." Fathers Ray Brown and John P. Meier speculate that the two apostles or Paul at least, may have been "denounced by extremely conservative Jewish Christian zealots."[43] It is hard to imagine that the net thrown out to catch Paul would not also have taken his fellow missionary apostle, Peter, if he was in the city at the time. That would have left the

---

[41] AA 15
[42] See *Dictionary of the Bible*, John L. McKenzie, S.J.; Bruce; Milwaukee, 1968; article "Peter"
[43] *Antioch & Rome: New Testament Cradles of Catholic Christianity*, Raymond E. Brown and John P. Meier; Paulist Press; NY; 1983; p. 212

Roman church a highly conservative and strongly Jewish Christian church well past the turn of the first century, which is what appears to have happened.

From all we know about Peter, he seems a hapless figure. Destined for greatness, he does not live up to his early promise. He slips from the scene leaving very little evidence of his passing. A generation has to elapse before Peter and Paul are acknowledged in Rome as "the greatest and most righteous pillars of the church."[44]

Nowhere in all of this history and literature does Peter exercise a monarchical leadership. His leadership is charismatic, visionary, full of prayer, and respectful of others. After the death of Jesus, he is no longer headstrong. Instead he doubts himself. His entire reliance is on the Lord dwelling within him whom he speaks with in prayer and whose power he shows forth in miracles. Peter has emptied himself out for the following of Jesus Christ.

Matthew is thought to have written his gospel in and for the church of Antioch probably in the 80s. Peter has been dead for 20 years or more. The Antioch church is undergoing tensions, probably between Jewish Christians and gentile Christians. In addition to questions about keeping kosher, the Jews, whose nation had lost the war against the Romans in 70 CE and who suffered from the destruction of their capital city, Jerusalem, were probably suspected by gentiles as 'subversives,' people not to be trusted. In this crisis, Matthew writes his gospel in part to bring together the two disparate factions and possibly also to solve some problems of authoritarian leadership that are beginning to assert themselves in the community, problems that would raise their head a generation later in the person of Ignatius of Antioch and his urgent campaign for monarchical bishops.

Matthew relies on the community's memories of Peter, memories that would later be preserved by Luke in the Acts of the Apostles, to remind them of a gentle, visionary church leader who was equally devoted to both Jews and Gentiles. He has Jesus say, "You are Peter, and upon this rock, I will build my community," 'community' or 'gathering' being other ways to translate the word *ekklesía*, commonly translated as 'church.'

---

[44] 1 Clem. 5:2

But to make certain that he is praising Peter for his character as a moderating presence–and <u>not</u> as an authority figure– Matthew, two chapters later in his narrative, attributes the same power of binding and loosing to the lay people in the community. Speaking about a brother who sins against another member of the community, Matthew describes the various approaches to the erring brother. Only as a last resort is he to be excluded from the community. As justification, he records Jesus saying to the ordinary members of the community, the lay people,

> "Amen, I say to you, whatever you bind on earth shall be bound in heaven and whatever you loose on earth shall be loosed in heaven. Again I say to you, if two of you agree on earth about anything for which they are to pray, it shall be granted to them by my heavenly Father. For where two or three are gathered together in my name, there am I in the midst of them." (Mt 18:18-20)

Matthew himself is not about to let leadership of the Christian community be wrested out of the hands of ordinary people by dominating leaders.

Yet the church's later hierarchs have relied on the myth of Peter as the first bishop of Rome, i.e., pope, as the sole basis on which to rest their overweening ambitions to rule all Christianity. They rely on vapor and smoke–and their own chutzpah. Having cooked up this myth, they interpret Jesus' words to Peter in a crassly political sense, instead of a human and spiritual sense, while ignoring Matthew's full gospel.

In fact, if Peter died in Nero's persecution of 64 CE, his body was probably tossed into a pit along with the bodies of other Christians or set afire.[45] Fathers Brown and Meier speculate that he was betrayed by others in the Roman Christian community. I will point out the obvious: Who would be in a position to be "jealous"– the Greek word used of those responsible for the betrayal of Peter and Paul–or to have had an "unholy zeal,"–another equally justified translation of the same phrase–if not the existing leaders of the Jewish Christian community in Rome?

---

[45] *Dictionary of the Bible*, John L. McKenzie, S.J.; Bruce; Milwaukee, 1968; article "Peter"

So today's leaders of the Roman Christian community are capitalizing on a crime of their predecessors. How apt!

> "Woe to you, scholars of the law. Your fathers slew the prophets and you build their monuments. Thus you approve the acts they did. They killed them and you do the building." (Cf. Lk 11:47-48)

and

> "Behold, I send to you prophets and wise men and scribes; some of them you will kill and crucify, some of them you will scourge in your gatherings and pursue from town to town, so that there may come upon you all the righteous blood shed upon earth, from the righteous blood of Abel to the blood of Zechariah, the son of Barachiah, whom you murdered between the sanctuary and the altar. Amen, I say to you, all these things will come upon this generation." (Mt 23:34-36)

Jesus Christ condemns the religious leaders of Rome just as he condemned the religious leaders of Jerusalem and for the same reasons. Is it any wonder that John Paul II's leader of the Congregation for the Doctrine of the Faith (CDF), successor to the Grand Inquisitor, avoided all mention of the historical Jesus, except to demean those who put their faith in him?

John Allen, in his book, *Cardinal Ratzinger: The Vatican's Enforcer of the Faith*, recounts one of the few instances when Cardinal Ratzinger[46] addressed the question of the historical Jesus:

> Ratzinger rejects the "common view" that Jesus acted as a prophet, offering a critique of an overly rigorous approach to the law. "In Jesus' exchange with the Jewish authorities of his time, we are not dealing with a confrontation between a liberal reformer and an ossified traditionalist hierarchy," Ratzinger said. This reading "fundamentally misunderstands the conflict of the New Testament and does justice neither to Jesus nor to Israel."... [T]he conflict between Jesus and the Israelite religious

---

[46] Later 'elected' Pope Benedict XVI.

establishment is over his acting *ex auctoritate divina*, in other words, his claim to be God.[47]

Notice how Ratzinger ignores the massive weight of New Testament evidence that attributes the Chief Priests' antagonism to Jesus as arising out of Jesus' being uncontrollable, a prophet, a religious reformer, not deferring to their power. Instead, Ratzinger finds the theological needle in the haystack that appeals to him. 'Their antagonism to Jesus came from his calling himself God.' It's true that this comes close to being one of the allegations made against him at his 'trial.' Most Catholic scripture scholars, however, believe that the full meaning of Jesus calling himself God's son was not recognized by the Christian community until after the resurrection. Ratzinger is grasping at straws. Give him full points for supercilious arrogance, though. He made the argument at a Jewish-Christian conference in Jerusalem where the very assertion of this point was bound to emphasize the differences between Jews and Christians and not their common ground.

Forgive me if I make doubly sure that Ratzinger doesn't get away with that travesty of New Testament interpretation:

Refutation of Ratzinger's Guess About Why Jesus Was Crucified

Mark's version of why Jesus was crucified has Jesus making a triumphal entry into Jerusalem, and shortly after that he cleanses the Temple.

> Then he taught them, saying, "Is it not written: 'My house shall be called a house of prayer for all peoples'? But you have made it a den of thieves."
>
> The chief priests and the scribes came to hear of it and were seeking a way to put him to death; yet they feared him because the whole crowd was astonished at his teaching. (Mk 11:17-19)

Toward the end of that chapter of Mark, Jesus returns to the Temple area, and "the chief priests, the scribes, and the elders

---

[47] *Cardinal Ratzinger: The Vatican's Enforcer of the Faith*, by John L. Allen, Jr.; Continuum; NY; 2000; p. 312

approached him and said to him, 'By what authority do you do these things? Or who gave you this authority to do them? '"

When they are unwilling to answer his counter-question, whether John the Baptist's Baptism was of heavenly or of human origin, he declines to answer their question about his authority. Instead, in chapter 12 immediately following, he tells the parable of a man who builds a vineyard and leases it out to tenants. When he sends servants to collect a portion of the yield as rent, the tenants treat them shamefully. When he sends his son to collect from the tenants, they reason, "Let us kill the heir, and the inheritance will be ours." And so they do. Jesus continues:

> "What will the owner of the vineyard do? He will come, put the tenants to death, and give the vineyard to others.
>
> "Have you not read this scripture passage:
>
> "'The stone that the builders rejected has become the cornerstone;
>
> "'by the Lord has this been done, and it is wonderful in our eyes'?"
>
> They were seeking to arrest him, but they feared the crowd, for they realized that he had addressed the parable to them. So they left him and went away. (Mk 11:27-12:12)

Again at the beginning of chapter 14, Mark says,

> So the chief priests and the scribes were seeking a way to arrest him by treachery and put him to death. They said, "Not during the festival, for fear that there may be a riot among the people." (Mk 14:1-2)

As to the motives of the chief priests, the scribes, and the elders, what could be clearer? Jesus is a religious reformer. He is a challenge to their authority. He has a following among the people, and the religious leadership fear him for it. You can't get much more political than that. He says his opinion is important because he is the son of the owner of the vineyard of Israel. And people half-believe him. They want to hear more.

The chief priests, the scribes, and the elders don't care about his claims. They care only about the threat he poses to their position in the religious state of Israel. If they DID care about his claims, they would instead want to hear more. They would listen attentively, as the Jews did after the resurrection, and their reaction would be similar:

> Now when they [the Jews of Jerusalem] heard this, they were cut to the heart, and they asked Peter and the other apostles, "What are we to do, my brothers?" (AA 2:37)

Instead, the chief priests, the scribes, and the elders are intent on tricking Jesus into some statement that they can call blasphemous, because blasphemy earns the penalty of death in their religious law, and they know they can get the Romans to put him to death under a civil disobedience charge.

I chose the gospel of Mark because Mark was closer in time to the actual events. Matthew and Luke have similar gospels, but they often confuse the story by including the Pharisees among Jesus' adversaries. The Pharisees were not Jesus' true opponents. He disputed with them about matters of religious governance and other religious matters only because he usually could not directly confront the religious leaders of Israel. He talked over the heads of the scribes and the Pharisees, so to speak, to the actual Jewish leadership. Some of the Pharisees only become true opponents of Christianity after Jesus' death.

The confrontation in the Temple is one of the few instances where Jesus does directly oppose "the chief priests and the elders of the people." Matthew's gospel portrays the opposition even more starkly. He adds another parable, the parable of the two sons. A father says to one of his sons, "Son, go out and work in the vineyard today." The son says, "No," but later he relents and goes out and works. The second son, when asked, says, "Yes, sir," but he does not go. Jesus then asks,

> "Which of the two did his father's will?" They (the chief priests and elders) answered, "The first." Jesus said to them, "Amen, I say to you, tax collectors and prostitutes are entering the kingdom of God before you.
>
> "When John came to you in the way of righteousness, you did not believe him; but tax collectors and prostitutes did. Yet even when you saw that, you did not later change your minds and believe him." (Mt 21:28-32)

Matthew, like Mark, follows this parable with the parable of the tenants and concludes with a similar statement.

When the chief priests and the Pharisees heard his parables, they knew that he was speaking about them. And although they were attempting to arrest him, they feared the crowds, for they regarded him as a prophet. (Mt 21:45-46)

Though Matthew began his account like Mark talking about the "chief priests and the elders," he ends, unlike Mark, talking about the "chief priests and the Pharisees." The Pharisees have become a problem for Matthew's church at Antioch. That, however, does not weaken the force of Jesus' attack: it is against the religious leadership of his time.

It is true, as Ratzinger says, that Jesus insisted upon his unique position as God's spokesman to Israel when making his case for the kingdom of God. But it is not true–in fact, it is ridiculous–that he was killed because of his theology. He was killed because of his politics. Not just Mark and Matthew, but the gospel of John is quite clear on that point:

> [At a meeting of the Sanhedrin, one of the members says] "What are we going to do? This man is performing many signs. If we leave him alone, all will believe in him, and the Romans will come and take away both our land and our nation."
>
> But one of them, Caiaphas, who was high priest that year said to them, "You know nothing, nor do you consider that it is better for you that one man should die instead of the people, so that the whole nation may not perish." (Jn 11:47-50)

That's not theology; that's politics. Isn't it odd that Cardinal Ratzinger, on his way to the papacy, occupied for us the place of Caiaphas–he is the one who silences the prophetic voice. And this present Roman hierarchy have put themselves in a position identical to the position of those who killed Jesus.

"You Hypocrites!"

Our church was founded by a person who was thoroughly angry with the religious leadership of his time. That much is clear from the gospels. Much of the time, he seems to be criticizing the scribes and the Pharisees, but they were only the enablers of the religious establishment. They were the fellow travelers. At a time when the religious leadership kept hired gangs in their employ[48] and were quite capable of murdering their opponents,[49] he had to be careful about naming them directly. But the priestly leadership were the real objects of his invective. And they realized, when they heard certain of his parables, that he was actually talking about them, about their stewardship of the religion of Israel.

And the term he used for the religious leaders and their surrogates, 'hypocrites,' may well have made them especially angry. The gospels show us Jesus using that term 17 times against the religious leaders of his day. Historically, the term has been left untranslated. Hypocrite is simply a transliteration of the Greek word, *hypokritēs*. A *hypokritēs* was a 'play-actor,' with just that tone of derision that the phrase has for us today. Because of the way the term was used in the gospels, it came to mean someone who pretends to be what he isn't in religion. Someone who pretends to be holy when, in fact, he isn't holy at all; he's a hypocrite.

What the Jews understood by that term may have been even more serious. Many of the Jews may have believed the high priesthood was illegitimate. The last legitimately appointed high priest was Onias II who was forced out of office in 175 BCE.[50] After that, the Maccabees, who were not of high priestly lineage– i.e., descended from King David's high priest, Zadok–assumed the office and began the Hasmonean line of high priests. This happened in 152 BCE and is thought to have been the occasion when the *hasidim*, later known as the Essenes, retired to the desert in protest against the now illegitimate high priesthood.[51]

Jesus seems to have coined this term of reproof. If he didn't coin it, he gave the term a meaning and a pungency that have lasted down through the ages. Applied to the high priesthood, it may well have meant that the high priests were participating in a fiction. They had the Temple as a stage, they had the priestly

---

[48] *Jerusalem in the Time of Jesus*; Joachim Jeremias; Fortress; Philadelphia; 1967; p. 106, pp. 105f

[49] Mt 23:34-36

[50] *Jerusalem*; p. 184

[51] *The New Jerome Biblical Commentary*; eds Raymond E. Brown, S.S., Joseph A. Fitzmyer, S.J., and Roland E. Murphy, O.Carm.; Prentice Hall; Englewood Cliffs, NJ; 1990; 26:38

vestments, they made their entrances and exits on cue, they knew their lines. But they were not high priests. Their 'play' was intended to deceive a nation.

And they were well paid for their performance. The Temple treasury was filled by devout Jews throughout the world.

This makes Jesus' words much more serious when he says,
"Is it not written: 'My house shall be called a house of prayer for all peoples'? But you have made it a den of thieves." (Mk 11:17)

He overturns the tables of the moneychangers as a symbolic act of cutting off the flow of money into the Temple governed by an illegitimate high priesthood. No wonder they decided to kill him!

Now the scriptures are not just historical documents. Their meaning is intended as instruction for all times. If it is true that the Christian priesthood originated, not with Jesus Christ nor any of the apostles, but sometime after the first century CE, further that it was a creation of the church intended as a matter of efficiency to concentrate its religious administration in the hands of a class of specialists, following the examples of religious priesthoods throughout the ancient world, and that later it acquired a mystique that set it entirely apart from the rest of the church and allowed the priesthood so formed to separate itself from control by, and answerability to, the rest of the church–if these things are true, as I maintain they are–then we have a situation very similar to the one Jesus faced.

Here was and is a group of people receiving respect (and money) to which they are not entitled and exercising authority that was and is entirely spurious. The parallel is startling. But the worst of it is, today they are pretending to be God, on the one hand, and interfering in our relationship with God, on the other.

This is a *kairós*, an acceptable time, a God-given opportunity, for the Catholic faithful to become true disciples (i.e., students) of Jesus Christ. It is up to us to re-learn our heritage and reclaim it from the hirelings and unjust stewards who pose as our leaders now.

What About the Priests?

Our complaint is with the priesthood as a tool of the hierarchy, not with individual priests. How can we complain, after all, about all of the good priests we have known throughout the years, priests who have taught and inspired us, who have led us to look beyond the mere appearance of things, to aim at knowledge, and at more than that–wisdom, to know and to love God and our fellow human beings? These men have acted, not only as teachers, but as counselors, confessors, supporters in times of trouble, and many of them as friends. They have baptized our children, married us, anointed our sick, buried our dead, and especially brought us the Mass. This revolution must make every effort to spare them from harm. They are, after all, even greater victims of the hierarchy than are the laity. More than that, for every priest who is willing to work alongside us, we must find a place.

For that reason, I can only hope that the full transition from today's church to the church of the future will last at least a generation. That will give us time to meld together all of the church's resources, both clerical and lay. We have a number of big jobs ahead of us. We must introduce the great multitude of Catholics to the true origins of their faith, reintroduce them to Jesus Christ and the fullness of his message. We must adapt the church's institutions to more lay-centered concerns, to convert the seminaries, for instance, into facilities for training the laity in the faith, to rearrange church structures so as to be able to free the clergy and the laity for more productive enterprises in the church. For these tasks, many of the clergy are well equipped and, in fact, anxious for a chance to remodel this top-heavy church. It cannot be very fulfilling for them simply to serve as symbols of hierarchical authority in the foreign seas of the laity. They are good for more than just showing the flag of a false monarchy.

More than that, many who spent their entire lives in the priesthood have already prepared the way for this revolution, some in works of great scholarship, others in their clear unanimity with the cause of the laity. We owe them a debt of gratitude, one we can repay only by faithfulness to our cause. Many of them have watched with the same alarm as we the rolling back of all of the reforms launched by the Second Vatican Council. They have felt the same helplessness as we but have carried the additional burden of defending the church hierarchy, when they knew in their hearts that all of the hierarchy's moves were against the Spirit of the church.

Obviously, when this revolution begins, Catholic priests will be caught in the middle. Our action will be "a sign that will be contradicted...which will reveal the hearts of many,"[52] especially in the clergy. Some will ally themselves with the hierarchy and oppose us. Others and perhaps the great majority will sympathize with what we are doing. It will be dangerous for these sympathizers to give any indication of their sentiments. We will have to trust in their prayers and good wishes and continue with our plans. In effect, though, these silent ones will be our fifth column. They may provide us with much good information which will help in transforming the existing structures of the church.

Once again I am stunned by the close parallel between our experience now and the experience of the early church:

- A high priesthood, jealous of its power, attempts to enforce discipline and root out dissent wherever it appears, crucifying and imprisoning the prophetic voice.
- Once the revolution starts, many in the lower priesthood recognize the hand of God and join with the laity in the new movement–just as in the early church.
- The movement for reform within the church has to deal continually with reconciling older practices, like Torah observance/canon law, with new insights provided by the Holy Spirit.
- The future of the new movement remains inscrutable to those who are a part of it; they cannot tell what shape the future 'church' will have.

The future of the Catholic church *is* inscrutable. We need not worry about that. Our job is simply to follow the Holy Spirit. We can do this only if we *believe* in the Holy Spirit. Once you trust yourself to its (his, her) leadership, the rest is easy. Jesus once said, "Don't let your heart be troubled. You believe in God; believe also in me."[53] Now he is saying, "Don't let your heart be troubled. You

---

[52] Lk 2:34-35
[53] Jn 14:1

believe in me; believe also in the Holy Spirit whom I have sent you as I promised."

"The world as we see it is passing away," said St. Paul.[54] It certainly must have felt that way to a highly observant Pharisee, converted only by a miracle to recognize these hated Jewish sectarians as possessing the fuller truth and to recognize their dead leader as the promised Messiah. Paul was compelled to admit that the basic assumptions of his faith–the death of prophecy and its substitution by study and observance of the Law–were false. Then as now, prophecy was not dead; it was simply ground underfoot by overweening authority–unsuccessfully, as it turns out. Paul, the most rigorous enforcer of the Law, himself became a prophet. Who knows, there may yet be hope for those like Cardinal Ratzinger.

---

[54] 1 Cor 7:31

The Current Crisis and Democracy in the Catholic Church

> THESE are the times that try men's souls. The summer soldier
> and the sunshine patriot will, in this crisis, shrink from the
> service of their country; but he that stands it now, deserves the
> love and thanks of man and woman. Tyranny, like hell, is not
> easily conquered; yet we have this consolation with us, that
> the harder the conflict, the more glorious the triumph. What
> we obtain too cheap, we esteem too lightly: it is dearness only
> that gives every thing its value. Heaven knows how to put a
> proper price upon its goods; and it would be strange indeed if
> so celestial an article as FREEDOM should not be highly
> rated.
>
> –Thomas Paine, *The Crisis*

The time has come for us Catholics to take the labor of the church upon ourselves, to take up our cross and follow Christ. It *will* be a nuisance, but that is the price of freedom. It has been comfortable all these years to let George or John Paul or Benedict do it, but they have now gone so far astray that it will require radical measures to gather them back in again. They have to learn that God is in charge, that he has not left us orphans, that the Holy Spirit is alive and well among the laity, despite the hierarchy's lack of faith in that Spirit. We have successfully dispelled the notion of the divine right of kings. It is time now to dispel the idea of the divine right of popes. It is time for a return–if not to democracy, then to the *sensus fidelium*–in the church.

What are we up against? First of all, the church is made up of many kinds of people, and the current crisis is affecting them in different ways.

- *The simply devout*, who are preoccupied with their devotions and with prayer, have the faith of children. These are the ones the current leadership considers 'the simple faithful.' The hierarchy don't wish to disturb their faith. Of course not! These are the people who trust the hierarchy implicitly. Their faith is in the leadership who have taught them to be docile. They have yet to experience life in Christ as development, growth, and change.

- *The great mass of the laity*, who are fully engaged in the work of the world, trying to fulfill the obligations of their state of life, trying to earn a living, master their craft, care for their children, and in general improve the world as they find it. For them their religion is a source of comfort–or would be if only they could feel reassured about the church as they encounter it. In the Third World, the laity are restrained by their poverty and, often, by the oppression of government leaders, wealthy landowners, and other economic interests from doing more than eking out an existence. For them, their religion is a lifeline to a better life. Many of the laity would be more fully engaged in the church as the following of Jesus Christ if they were not taught to be fully dependent on the presence of a clergyman to validate their sacramental life as Christians.

- *The priests, the lower clergy* including those bishops who have very little contact with the ruling powers of the church. Many of these are discouraged, even greatly demoralized, by the current scandals in the church and by the loss of support they feel from both the hierarchy and the laity. The hierarchy have been forced by their own misdeeds and by the ensuing loss of financial support to cut programs and reduce or eliminate many of the ministries that priests have formerly carried out. From the laity, priests sense the loss of the automatic approval they received in the past.

- *Religious men and women.* While their numbers have fallen appreciably, they remain an important stabilizing influence in the church. Their long history of service to the church usually helps them avoid the full force of oppressive Vatican directives. But not always. For example, in 1981, the pope prevented the Jesuits from electing their own superior general. The pope did not like their support for liberation theology. For two years, he put in his own choice for their superior until a candidate acceptable to him could be elected. Religious communities are important to the Catholic church for another reason. Living in community, they are able to imitate the early church as depicted in the New Testament book of Acts. Third, some religious communities can trace their history at least as far back as the current hierarchy of the church; in fact, there are religious communities that antedate the coining of the term hierarchy in the sixth century. One religious community, the Carmelites, claims to trace its origins back before New Testament times, which may be mythology, but may not be able to be disproved or proved. In any case, religious communities continue as an important 'third force' in the church.

- *The Opus Dei clergy and laity*, a recently founded secret society in the Official Catholic Church, whose aim is to support their own leaders and their conservative view of the church without question. Opus Dei members are a troubling element in the church because of their unthinking obedience to the will of their leaders and because of the secrecy of their operations. They are in effect active agents of totalitarianism within the church. The present hierarchy strongly supports them. It has canonized their founder, and is scheming to bring Opus Dei clergy into the leadership of the church.
- *The hierarchy,* all those who currently dominate the church. They include the pope, the Curia, the cardinals, and all those bishops who agree with this system.

The current crisis is one of leadership. There is no doubt about who leads the Official Catholic Church. It is the pope. Everyone who feels he owes the pope strict obedience, anyone who can be removed from office by the pope, or anyone who looks to the pope for preferment or simply as the ruler of the church–anyone like this is a part of the Official Catholic Church. This includes all of the hierarchy and, unfortunately, all of those among the clergy and the laity who look upon the pope as the vicar of Christ and the successor of St. Peter.

For others in the clergy and for many of the laity, however, Jesus Christ is the head of the church, and the pope is supposed to be his follower. What these people may not realize, though, is that the pope and the hierarchy cannot simply be ignored. They are a divisive force. Never in their history have the hierarchy been a stabilizing force–unless the stability looked for was one that simply maintained them in office regardless of the consequences. The papacy and the hierarchy are responsible for the fact that at times we have had two or three rival popes. Often the pope, supposedly the bishop of Rome, was not elected by the Romans and did not live in Rome at all. For 70 years, the pope ruled from Avignon in France. In technical, theological, terms, the pope and the hierarchy are a scandal. They distract from the leadership of Jesus Christ, and they block the spread of the gospel. As one of many examples, they destroyed the China mission established with great wisdom by Matteo Ricci in the late 16th and early 17th centuries. China could well have developed a strong Catholic church–except for the Roman hierarchy! And how different our history might be today!

The great mass of the faithful, and many of the clergy, are caught in the middle. They feel conflicted about the church, but they don't know why. These are the ones who, in Jesus' words are, "like sheep without a shepherd." Included in this number are all of those alienated from the church for one reason or another who still consider themselves Catholics.

Meanwhile, the Holy Spirit is guiding the church unerringly. From the papacy of John XXIII, when gales of fresh air filled the church, to the present day, Rome has surreptitiously closed the windows, locked them, installed iron gratings across them, and defied anyone to open them again. The atmosphere inside the Official Catholic Church is stifling. It is as if God wanted to remind his people of the freshness of his spirit, knowing what our reaction would be when it was taken away.

The Spirit has been taken away–or has departed–from the institutional church. It has not been taken away from the church at large. God has given us the gift of understanding. He has given us the gift of immediate and unmediated access to himself. He has given us all the power we need to rectify what is now going on in the Official Catholic Church. And I believe God is asking us not to abuse the tremendous power we have: for it is within our power to do away with the Official Catholic Church entirely by withholding our funding. And we can rebuild the church again simply by not refusing our communion to those who wish to change their allegiance from the current false hierarchy to the Catholic church being revived through Lay Catholic Renewal.

But there should be no misunderstanding about our resolve. Make up your mind to it, you Catholic lay people: we must not contribute to hierarchy with no strings attached. If they are willing to spell out what they want funds for–in detail–then each of us can consider lending our support. For hierarchy pure and simple, there should be no support. We must never contribute to the misconception that there is a class of people, not chosen by us in the Holy Spirit, who nonetheless have been divinely ordained to be our leaders. Unfortunately, we will have to guard against lies. Since the founding myth of the papacy is a lie, pure and simple, and a whopper, we know that the hierarchy are fully capable of telling big lies with a straight face, what we in the Midwestern United States would call, 'bald-face, bucket-mouth lies.'

Peter's Pence, for instance, goes to support the bureaucracy that weighs us down. The pope's biggest charity is himself and his court. It has become widely known that when he travels to foreign countries he places an enormous financial burden on the dioceses he visits. For some dioceses, it takes years to recover. This has nothing to do with the following of Jesus Christ. It is a distraction from Jesus Christ. It creates a cult of personality around one who says he takes the place of Christ, who is trying to establish Christ's kingdom on earth—yet our Lord said, "My kingdom is not of this world." Shame on the pope! If he wishes to travel, let him travel like any other human being. Let him imitate the Jesus Christ whose place he claims to take.

The current crisis in the Catholic church is also one of freedom–freedom for all of the groups mentioned above, the freedom of the children of God (Rom 8:21). Some of those above are working hard against freedom for the other members of the church. They are misguided. They do not understand our heritage. They do not understand the gospel. I'm sure we reached this pass because the great mass of the church trusted that their fellow Catholics would never act so decidedly against their brothers' and sisters' interests. Once the reign of authority began, however, there was no lack of theoreticians and apologists to argue in its favor. That is how we accumulated the vast reservoir of human traditions invented to support the papacy. Those traditions are all dust and ashes, misspent effort, sound and fury signifying nothing.

"From the beginning, it was not so" (Mt 19:8). This principle of the Lord's will carry us through every revision of the structure and disposition of the Catholic church, provided only that we pay attention to the Holy Spirit. Without the Holy Spirit who inspires us to interpret it, all scripture is mute, silent, without significance. The principle, 'From the beginning it was not so,' will help us in deciding what is essential to our faith, what is useful, and what is distracting or even counterproductive. Another principle of the Lord's will be equally helpful: "Every scribe learned in the Kingdom of Heaven is like a householder who brings out of his storeroom things new and old" (Mt 13:52). We are not to limit ourselves to a slavish imitation of any presumed ideal of the early church, for instance, but are to follow the promptings of the Spirit who will adapt the church perfectly for our time.

Also, I would not presume to lay out a blueprint for the future church. I can provide only that portion of the divine plan that the Lord is gracious enough to share with me. My view shows me the local churches. How they will associate and what form their association will take, I leave to others whom the Spirit will choose. I know that the glue that holds them together will be the Holy Spirit.

I can imagine that they will have a loose union, and that representatives chosen by the churches will meet together to discuss matters of common interest. That they will ever fall into disputes about whose church is greater, or whose church should be subject to whose, I can't imagine. We should learn something from the church's past mistakes, just as we should take advantage of its insights.

I know for certain only that the Lord has rejected the current structure and has declared it no longer valid. The Lord demands a return to a simpler model, one that will bring God closer to his people–(please forgive the pronouns)–and make possible an earlier union with others of his followers. I see the future church as more of a brother-and-sisterhood, one that does not make demands but tries to cooperate, one that is concerned for all humankind and does its best to lift up the downtrodden. One that tries to imitate the Christ who announced his mission in the words

> The Spirit of the Lord is upon me,
> because he has anointed me
> to bring glad tidings to the poor.
> He has sent me to proclaim liberty to captives
> and recovery of sight to the blind,
> to let the oppressed go free,
> to proclaim a year acceptable to the Lord. (Lk 4:18-19)

As the Prophet says, 'For every thing, there is a season:... a time to tear down and a time to build' (Ecles 3:1,3). I strongly feel that this is a time to build. Another metaphor may apply. If you have a choice of irrigating a field with worn out soil, full of dead roots and overgrown with trees that suck the water from the crops and overshadow them so that they cannot grow to maturity, or, on the other hand, irrigating a fresh field with good soil, full of sunlight, ripe for sowing–where would you put your water and your effort? Let us permit the 'field' of the hierarchy to become desiccated while we water the local churches.

Democracy in the Church: How Would It Work?

The Catholic equivalent of democracy in the church ought to be the *sensus fidelium*. The *sensus fidelium* is the theological notion of the common understanding of the faithful. It is the essential requirement to be taken into account before any dogma is defined. It is a requirement, needless to say, more honored in the breach than in the observance.

The idea behind this doctrine is that you cannot say what the Catholic church believes without first knowing, for a fact, what the church–that is, the people–actually do believe. It is the equivalent of turning to a group of people and asking, "Isn't that your understanding?"

It implies several underlying truths. The first is the vital importance of the grassroots, the ordinary people who make up the church, as witnesses to what the Holy Spirit teaches. The next is mutual courtesy, kindness, consideration. The next is servant-leaders who are truly servants of the community and NOT people who make decisions on their own without consulting the community.

In a house church, even with a varying group of attendees, if everyone is treated courteously, and the principles of *Sharing Wisdom* are used to make decisions (See the next chapter on the technique of shared decision making), we will be able to elect leaders whom we can delegate for various tasks just as in the early church. The earliest church had prophets and teachers and elders, not as leaders, but as servants of the community. They ministered to it. And when the need was felt to evangelize other communities, apostles were sent to those other communities. (The meaning of the term apostle is "one who is sent forth.") Typically these apostles came from among the prophets and teachers of the community. This kind of cross-pollination from one community to another will be important to the success of Lay Catholic Renewal.

As anyone who has ever participated in, say, an informal study group knows, a group of people who gather together periodically without inspiring social and intellectual nourishment, without stated goals to be achieved within a given period of time, and without varying the membership and the leadership of the group–such a group will grow stale. In our house churches, we will not have the threat of persecution to test our adherence to Christ. We will have to task ourselves to live the gospel as the Spirit lays its demands upon us.

Part of the problem may be that we have become couch potatoes. We watch television. We watch sporting events. We watch the Mass. We are called 'cafeteria Catholics.' Instead of actively living life, we passively watch life go by. We are like the lukewarm people mentioned in the Book of Revelation (Rv 3:15-16). We are enervated. We will feel much better about ourselves and our faith if we become more conscious of our beliefs and more active in our local church. It ought to matter that we are Catholics. The old paradigm of 'Pay, pray, and obey' is dead, but it's going to take work to replace it with real adherence to Jesus Christ.

The early church did not have an imposing superstructure of leadership. We need not either. The ability to meet and exchange ideas vicariously over the Internet is a blessing from God. This is a significant advantage for us in what would otherwise be an unequal struggle against an opposition that already occupies the ground, so to speak. Another advantage, however, is the sympathy we will have from a great many clergy and religious who will see the merit in our arguments and recognize instinctively and from experience the huge disparity between the movement begun by Jesus Christ and the present Roman Catholic church.

The revival of the Catholic church requires the empowerment of lay Catholics in a return to the practices of the early church. It does not necessarily mean the disempowerment of the clergy. In fact, in the interim, it may mean the empowerment of bishops and clergy alike in the face of monarchical Roman claims. Though the situation is not quite the same, the early church did have a fair number of priests among its adherents. All of the church together, without distinction, believed Jesus was the Messiah and expectantly awaited his return.

This glad expectation of the coming of Christ had a great leveling effect in the early church and was one reason why rich and poor, priests and lay people, Greek-speaking and Aramaic-speaking Jews, and eventually Jews and Gentiles got along fairly well together. The absence of that expectation in the Roman Catholic church today is one clear indication of the church's worldliness and inattention to the Spirit. The current leadership are completely consumed with their place in this world. They don't believe in the Master's return, and so, ironically, they have begun "to beat the menservants and the maidservants" (Lk 12:45).

It is important for our movement that we earn again the pagan accolade directed to the early Christian church, "See how [those Christians] love one another" (Tertullian, *Apology*, Ch. 39). I am reminded of an abortive attempt to form a lay Catholic organization in Chicago in 1970. The convening event was well publicized. My wife and I and a number of other Catholics active in our parish decided to attend. The meeting was held, I believe, in the gymnasium of St. Ignatius High School a mile or so from downtown Chicago. It was crowded. I remember recognizing a number of Big Catholics, i.e., lay people, professors, authors, and minor politicians, who had achieved a certain celebrity and who wore their Catholicism on their sleeve. I also noticed that quite a crowd of religious sisters, many in the habits of their sisterhoods, were filing in as well.

We entered the hall and took our places in the bleachers. On the floor of the gymnasium, a number of long tables had been set up for the group's organizers. There was a brief welcome. We learned that a steering committee had been chosen and a number of other committees selected. The names of the committee members were read out. I don't remember a ballot being passed or a vote being taken. The committees were asked to meet in the classrooms assigned to them.

Then followed a question-and-answer session. One of the questions concerned the religious sisters who had attended. Were they to be admitted to membership in the organization? The speaker did not hesitate with his answer. No, they would not be allowed to become members of the organization. They were religious, not lay people.

At that moment my jaw dropped. I looked at my wife in dumb disbelief. The lay Catholics who were setting up this organization didn't know the first thing about their own church. The societies of religious women, whether cloistered nuns or religious sisters, did not belong to religious "orders" as men's religious organizations were called. They had no status in canon law. Despite the fact that they had many more members than the men's religious orders and did far more work for the church, as far as Rome was concerned they were all lay people. To deny them membership in a group organized specifically for Catholic lay people was the height of ignorance in church matters–and injustice.

And the way the organization had been set up, without a single vote being taken, without any serious attempt to involve the lay people who had come to the founding meeting, was pure political ignorance. It was perfectly 'Catholic,' though, in the reactionary way in which it manipulated the laity. My esteem for Big Catholics, never very high, fell to a new low.

"This organization is going nowhere," I said to my wife. She agreed. We attended no further meetings, though there was at least one more.

Brothers and sisters, we must avoid this kind of buffoonery. We ought to know something about the church we belong to. And we should follow Jesus' lead in creating organizations with porous boundaries.

For instance, I don't understand homosexuality. At the same time, I have known homosexuals with whom I have cooperated and been on good terms and whose gifts and contributions to society I recognize and applaud. I don't like the idea of characterizing people by a sexual designation. To me that seems dehumanizing. We are much more than what part sexuality may play in our lives. And everyone deserves respect.

More important, we Christians are supposed to be a unique society, a band of brothers and sisters known, not for our sexuality or for any other characteristic, but for our love. And by love I do not mean physical love or shows of affection. Those are entirely too superficial. St. Paul has given us the classic definition of Christian love in the 13th chapter of 1 Corinthians, verses 4 through 9:

> Love is patient, love is kind; love doesn't envy. Love doesn't brag, is not proud, doesn't behave itself inappropriately, doesn't seek its own way, is not provoked, thinks no evil; doesn't rejoice in injustice, but rejoices with the truth; bears all things, believes all things, hopes all things, endures all things. Love never fails. Prophecies, will fail. Tongues will cease. Knowledge will be done away with. For we know in part, and we prophesy in part; but when that which is complete has come, then that which is partial will be done away with.

That is the quality of the society we are trying to create. It must not be mistaken for a weak society, a weak church.

Does a loving society exclude homosexuals? Here is where the Holy Spirit lifts us up. I don't have to decide that question. I don't have enough wisdom for that. Our mandate is not to exclude people; it is to bring them in. Just as among Jesus' first followers, he does not exclude people; if anything, they exclude themselves. We are all called to heroic sacrifice. We are called to obey the commands of the Spirit. So long as each of us does his or her best to follow the Spirit, Jesus will show us the way.[55]

---

[55] On the whole question of inclusiveness with respect to homosexuals, please see the remarkable article "Homosexuality and the Church: Scripture and Experience" by Luke Timothy Johnson in *The Commonweal* magazine (June 15, 2007). Johnson is Robert R. Woodruff Professor of New Testament at the

Since it is a society we wish to create, we must think in political terms. We can rise above politics only by understanding politics well enough not to be blocked by political realities. It was precisely because they did not understand the politics of the people they were trying to organize that those would-be founders of the Catholic lay organization in 1970 failed.

Catholics in the United States, and, I would guess, throughout the world, have a strong desire to be consulted about matters touching the church. In this country, we ordinarily think we should "have a vote" on questions affecting us. But voting may not be the very best way to go.

The reason for this is that voting makes winners and losers. In a close vote, nearly half of the people who will be affected by a decision have shown, in effect, that they are not in favor of it. When they lose the vote, they are apt to feel disaffected. In their hearts they may be saying, "Okay, you voted for this proposal;

Candler School of Theology, Emory University. The article points out that down through the ages, Christianity as actually practiced has never lived in precise accord with the Scriptures. We do not stone psychics and adulterers, as Leviticus prescribes. We tolerate divorce, clearly against Jesus' command. We engage in war, directly counter to Jesus' nonviolent stance. The demands of scripture have always been modified by the lived experience of human beings. But in some of our reinterpretation of scripture, we have been guided by the Holy Spirit.

Johnson says our situation with respect to the authority of scripture is like that of the 19th century American abolitionists. Scripture seemed to tolerate slavery. Slavery supporters could point to Galatians 3:28 and Paul's Letter to Philemon as seeming to accept it. But the lived experience of slavery's horror in this country, once it reached people's critical consciousness, turned the nation away from slavery. It also meant that we could never read the Bible in quite the same way again.

Johnson invokes "the basic Pauline principle that the Spirit gives life but the letter kills (2 Cor 3:6). And if the letter of Scripture cannot find room for the activity of the living God in the transformation of human lives, then trust and obedience must be paid to the living God rather than to the words of Scripture."

In short, God is working within the church and within society to clarify the words of scripture. We are learning something new that God is presenting to us. As Johnson says, "if holiness among heterosexuals includes fidelity, chastity, modesty, and fruitfulness, we can ask whether and how the same elements are present in same-sex love."

now you can carry it out." Except in societies long used to majority rule, voting does not necessarily tend to unify a community.

In the following of Christ, what counts is wisdom. Sister Mary Benet McKinney, OSB, has spelled out what I think is the very best method of decision making for any Catholic community. She has drawn on ancient Christian monastic practice to spell out a way of 'discernment of spirits' in making decisions. This is the subject of the next chapter.

Sharing Wisdom

If the base communities set up in the process of lay Catholic renewal are to succeed, they must have a method of self-governance that will see them through the difficult early stages of their existence. Such a method ought to reflect Jesus' call to enter the kingdom of God: "Come to me all you who labor and are heavily burdened and I will refresh you,...for my yoke is easy and my burden light."[56] Fortunately, such a method of Christian self-governance has recently been developed.

Sharing Wisdom is the title of a book on group decision making in the Catholic church by Mary Benet McKinney, a Chicago Benedictine sister. Unfortunately, the book is now out of print. I learned this wonderfully effective method from Sister Mary Benet's book and will try to reproduce the author's ideas in enough detail so that the technique and its spirit can be put into practice. If you can lay hands on a copy of the book itself, that would provide the very best introduction to shared decision making.

Before writing *Sharing Wisdom*, Sister Mary Benet worked for more than 20 years advising groups within the church, especially to facilitate one change called for by Vatican II–the devolution of decision making from the highest levels of the church to the lowest possible levels at which decisions can be made. She worked with diocesan pastoral councils, priests' senates, boards of education, parish councils, and school boards "to translate the theology of Vatican II into workable models" for decision making.

Her experience is that we Western Catholics have great difficulty with group decision making, because we were taught to settle questions by taking a vote! We use the parliamentary model of decision making. Fifty-one percent of the group can compel a decision. This makes winners and losers. It is more likely to produce friction than unanimity.

Sister Mary Benet concluded that the parliamentary model itself was producing a great deal of discord in the church–lay

---

[56] Mt 11:28-30

people who feel they are being frustrated by the veto power of the clergy, and pastors who feel there is no role left for them in the post-Vatican II church. Much of this dissension, she feels, is built into the parliamentary decision making process.

With that frustrating experience, she began searching for a model that was more suited to the building up of the church and less likely to lead to conflict. The method she developed was partly traditional and partly adapted from more modern insights.

Her method of decision making has its roots in the monastic tradition and in the New Testament idea of the discernment of spirits. Its fundamental insights are that no one receives from the Holy Spirit all of the wisdom in a given situation and that, conversely, everyone has a piece of the wisdom. What she added is the essentially Christian feminist perspective that uses the skills and insights of the group to include people rather than to weed them out.

The method she outlines for coming to a decision can be time-consuming initially, but it often achieves remarkable and unexpectedly effective results. The method is consensus. Instead of voting, the group discusses the topic until a solution emerges with which everyone in the group can agree. Everyone is asked to express his or her opinion on the matter. This means that people who would normally remain silent are required to give their considered opinion.

What results is a much fuller discussion than in the parliamentary model. No one is allowed to monopolize the discussion. All participants are encouraged to actively solicit the opinions of all other members of the group and to give those opinions their full attention. What helps in this endeavor is the group members' faith in Jesus' word, "Where two or three are gathered together, I am there in their midst." Sister Mary Benet emphasizes that we should not visualize Jesus as being in the center of the room, but actually present within each member of the group.

"He will live in our very beings–calling, forming, challenging, speaking, listening. Or, to put it another way, He will be using our ears, our voices, our minds and hearts to be His presence in and for His church." She quotes Scripture scholar Fr. Eugene

LaVerdiere: "The greatest presence of the Risen Lord is another human being."[57]

The Prerequisites Are Spiritual!

For Sister Mary Benet's shared decision making model to work, all those involved in boards and councils within the Catholic church must understand that they are called to *be* and to *build* church. In her own words:

> What I am trying to say is that the criteria for membership on boards and councils must include the following:
>
> - A willingness to recognize this call as a call to holiness and, out of this recognition, to commit one's energies to the process of growing in holiness
> - A willingness to see this call as a call to ministry and therefore to accept formation and training both in preparation for membership and as an expected part of the experience of being a board or council member.[58]

Needless to say, these criteria are not restricted to boards and councils. Anyone who becomes a member of a base community or a house church must take it upon himself or herself to recognize their call to personal holiness and to ministry in the gathering (church) that Jesus Christ founded. And you can't pursue either holiness or ministry without some formation and training.

The enabling prerequisites for shared decision making in the Catholic church are the pursuit of holiness and the willingness to minister. That's why Sister Mary Benet calls for reflective prayer both before and after a decision is made. Here are the elements of discernment as she finds them in the Catholic tradition:

> 1. The sincere desire of those involved to grow in holiness so as to allow the voice of the Spirit to be heard in their lives and in their hearts

---

[57] *Sharing Wisdom: A Process for Group Decision Making*; Mary Benet McKinney, O.S.B.; Tabor Publishing; Allen, TX; 1987; pp 11-12

[58] Op. cit., p. 39

2. The ability to "let go," the "holy indifference" referred to in the tradition...so as to be able to surrender to the voice of the Spirit when it is heard

3. The inclusion of prayer and solitude in the process, both as preparation for and as integral to the doing of discernment

4. The guidance of a spiritual leader or pastor to shepherd the discerners through the process

5. The sharing of all that the Spirit has revealed to each member of the group

6. The agreement among the members of the group either to work until consensus is reached or to agree with the majority decision.[59]

Not every decision made in a base community or house church will call for the employment of the shared decision making model. But once the group becomes accustomed to its use, the habit of prayerful, respectful, insightful decision making will become second nature to the members.

How Does It Work?

When a proposal arises calling for a decision by the group, there are three steps:

1. Gathering the data from the "professionals" and from those to be affected by the possible decision. "(Those to be affected by your decision have the right to share their wisdom with you *before* you make the decision.)"

2. Reflecting prayerfully on the data. "This is where analysis and synthesis take place in each person's understanding of the data. This step involves the effort of each member of the group to reflect on the data in terms of his or her lived experience and insights and to listen to the promptings of the Spirit in the depths of the heart."

---

[59] Op. cit., p. 42

3. Sharing the wisdom that results from the reflection. "Having reflected prayerfully and touched one's own wisdom, each member must now share that wisdom with the total group and listen to all the other members as they share their wisdom. This is where analysis and synthesis take place in the group thinking. The effort here is again to try to hear the wisdom of the Spirit coming through the wisdom being shared within the group."

"When the wisdom is shared, it becomes new data which then need to be identified, clarified, and nuanced so that the group can reflect on it and then share that reflection. Thus the cycle often needs to be repeated, perhaps many times, before the decision will be made."[60]

Once the data have been gathered, the person or persons making the proposal set it forth with as much clarity as possible. They discuss the circumstances that prompted it and the likely results of its adoption. Then the leader or facilitator of the group calls for prayerful reflection on the data. After each person has had time to reflect on the data in the light of his or her own lived experience, "praying through feelings, insights, knowledge, and reactions," the leader then asks the opinion of each member of the group. Each person in turn then gives his or her opinion. In the course of this opinion-giving or after it, questions are asked and answers given back and forth. Everyone must provide her or his piece of the wisdom.

At the end of this first round of discussion, the chair or leader of the group asks if there is a consensus. This can be done by a show of hands. If there is a consensus, the proposal is slated for adoption at the next meeting. If there is not a consensus, those opposed are asked to give reasons for their opposition. Discussion then continues, with each member of the group being asked to speak to the reasons raised in opposition. This discussion may elicit new data, which again should be prayerfully considered by the group through as many cycles as needed.

---

[60] Op. cit., p. 43f

Such a process can have several outcomes, depending on the urgency and the gravity of the matter at hand.

First, as to urgency, one rule of this process is that no decision can be reached at the same meeting where it is first discussed. This is to allow time for prayer and recollection and to forestall hasty decisions.

Second, if the decision is not urgent and agreement cannot be reached, the proposal may fail or be postponed for lack of a consensus.

Third, if the decision cannot be postponed or avoided and action one way or another will have to be taken at the next meeting, the chair then asks if there is some form of the decision on which all can agree. Discussion then proceeds on this topic. The agreement now being sought is one in which those who opposed the implementation of the decision in its original form will at least give the revised decision their grudging support. As the question is usually stated, "Can you live with this decision?" If they can, this is another possible outcome.

Fourth, if the group remains divided and not even minimal agreement is possible in an unavoidable and urgent matter, as a last resort a vote may be taken. While this may be considered a breakdown of the process, shared decision making has at least yielded the very fullest discussion of the matter at hand.

Sister Mary Benet cites instances where a view that was very much in the minority at the beginning of a discussion gains momentum and finally becomes the consensus decision. The reason for outcomes like this is no doubt to be attributed to the group's prayerful approach to the question at hand and the members' selflessness in putting forth and accepting ideas.

The Experience of Consensus

One of the advantages of shared decision making, in my experience, is that it sidesteps, or overwhelms, all of the very real personality conflicts, hidden agendas, pecking-order establishments, ego trips, and other irrelevancies that have been well documented by those who study "Group Dynamics." Shared decision making inverts the pecking order; it solicits the aid of the least talkative members of the group. It surfaces hidden agendas by demanding a full discussion of ALL relevant agendas. It tones down all the excesses of "personalities" by demanding that we treat one another as blessed to be striving together, in the Lord's presence, for the Lord's kingdom. And to ego it opposes humility and courtesy in the Lord's service.

The actual experience of consensus is much better than the worst-case, group-dynamics scenario suggested above. The worst cases tend to occur at the very beginning of a group's use of consensus decision making. That's when people don't really believe in the technique and have to have all their questions answered before they give it a try. That first use of the technique is also the period when shared decision making overcomes group dynamics.

After what may be an excruciating experience of the first use of the consensus model, the group's decision making tends to become miraculously smooth and swift. Why? Because after that first test, the people in this group know one another. They realize they share the same Spirit and have at least a minimal regard for one another. In theory, at least, they are guaranteed not to have their opinion overlooked. Later decisions become easy precisely because these particular people in this group are not suspicious of one another's motives. They know where each one is coming from. And they believe a little more fully that the Lord is present to see them through.

BUT...there is also a downside. To an outsider, to someone joining the group after the Armageddon of the first use of shared decision making, the prior members of the group may seem to be a clique, an in-group. They may seem to be operating with a hidden agenda!

That's because the prior members have been through the war of the introduction of consensus decision making, they know the rules, they know what to expect, and when the new member may have some very big questions about what's going on, about the seeming lack of lively debate for instance, the older members don't seem to have any questions at all. Obviously, there's a hidden agenda!

That means that the shared decision making process must be explained fully to any new members as the first order of business. If at all possible, they should be given formal training in its use. All of their questions should be answered fully. The new members should know that consensus decision making is like the flight of the bumblebee–in theory, it can't work. But it does, and better than the parliamentary model we're most used to. It most nearly duplicates the decision making that went on in the early church, when people who had pledged everything to God and to one another signified their assent simply by a nod of the head or a wave of the hand.

And by the way, consensus decision making–without the specifically Christian aspects–is the same method used by the members of NATO. It can't possibly work. But it does.

The Enabling Leader

The tradition of discernment in the Catholic church calls for a leader who is open to the Spirit, "who walks the spiritual journey with us–one who listens, questions, affirms, challenges, and calls."[61] This leader is the very opposite of an authoritarian. She or he is an enabler, a catalyst, a facilitator.

Jesus was and is our very best example of this kind of leader. He made it clear who among the disciples was his second in command–Peter. He even identified his second-rank leadership, James and John, by including them in events with Peter in which the other disciples were not included. And he punished no one. He did not penalize the initiatives his disciples showed in their common endeavor for the Kingdom of God, even when these initiatives did not agree with his view of the mission.

"Lord, look, there are two swords here."

"It is enough."

Obviously they were not sufficient to resist an armed assault by the authorities, but the disciples caught his drift. They knew they were not expected to take up the sword in his defense.

When the disciples were keeping the crowds away from Jesus, something he appreciated at times, he made an exception without criticizing anyone.

"Let the children come to me; do not prevent them, for the kingdom of God belongs to such as these."

---

[61] Op. cit., p. 55

When Jesus was letting the disciples know that his destiny was to go up to Jerusalem and be killed, Peter tried to dissuade him. This showed a critical lack of insight in one of his closest followers. It pained Jesus deeply, and he grew angry.

"Get behind me, Satan! Your thinking is of men, not of God!"[62]

James and John were especially difficult to control on occasion. They wished to call down fire from heaven on the cities that did not welcome them. They wanted to prevent another Israelite, not one of their group, from performing cures in Jesus' name. And they wanted to sit at Jesus' right and left hand when he came to power.

Jesus was able to find replies to all of this, replies that clarified his mission—and theirs. And ours.

The point of all of this is that Jesus remains the best leader today. We must remember his usual mildness, his foresight, but also his intense concern for the kingdom; that is, for what we today call the reign of God in the hearts of the faithful. The kingdom of God is nothing if it is not established in the hearts and minds of human beings.

During his time on earth, Jesus showed us three things about leadership. First, we can't avoid having leaders; leaders just naturally assert themselves, as did Peter and James and John. And servant-leaders, the kind that Peter became after the resurrection, help the church by enabling it to carry out its aims regardless of what happens to the leaders themselves, even if they lose the status they seemed destined for.

But—the second example Jesus gave us—in the church, leaders are not meant to give direction; they are to act as catalysts, servant-leaders, people who challenge us to listen to the Holy Spirit. Direction comes from on high, from Jesus who remains our only true leader. And he announces his directives through the whole community and through the prophetic voice. That's where the usefulness of consensus decision making arises—it surfaces the prophetic voice.

Third, as Jesus restrained the leaders of his group directly when they wanted to control or persecute people, or when, as in

---

[62] Mk 8:33

Peter's case, he wanted unwittingly to frustrate God's plan of salvation for humanity, so we as a church have the obligation to rein in, censure, or dismiss leaders who have become corrupt or incompetent.

Leaders are a necessary evil in the church, but they must be kept on a tight leash and must be compared frequently with our only true leader.

Leaders in the Base Communities

This applies to the meetings of our base communities as well. Our leaders should be servant-leaders. We want people who are deferential to the members of the group, but not passive-aggressive. The passive-aggressive leader disguises under a cloak of mildness and inactivity his unwillingness to cooperate with the expressed will of the community. He defers action on any initiatives he does not favor. Mild as he may be, he is a dictator.

We want leaders who are alive to the Holy Spirit, facilitators who can focus the group on the task at hand, who are accustomed to asking the opinion of the group, and who can benefit from criticism. Once a direction has been decided on, the leader should carry out the directive as promptly as possible. If problems occur, he or she should report back in a timely fashion and, if need be, again ask for direction.

Also, we should think of leadership as temporary and communal. Leaders should encourage the development of other leaders. In this, too, we can follow the example of St. Peter. In the beginning of the Book of Acts, he has a commanding position of leadership in the early church. But that situation changes. Why? Probably because, in his concentration on prayer and learning the will of his master, he was not anxious about maintaining his leadership position. When the time came to welcome Gentiles into the new movement, he had no qualms about leaving Jerusalem, the seat of power in the early church, and journeying to Antioch where the Gentile church was forming. He was not concerned when James, the brother of the Lord, took up the leadership of the early church. In fact, he probably encouraged him to do so.

Peter met with Paul for some weeks after Paul's conversion. And though the two personalities were probably very different and their backgrounds even more different, Peter did nothing to discourage Paul's initiatives. Later, when a dispute arose between Paul and Peter at Antioch, Peter humbly submits to Paul's criticisms. He does not recriminate, he does not call down anathemas, he turns the problem over to God and, in effect, gives us the gift of the Pauline mission to the Gentiles.

It is possible that Peter too, like Paul, traveled to Asia Minor and to Greece. Evidently, he reached Rome, the capital of the world at that time and a very unfamiliar place for a middle-aged Jewish fisherman who probably spoke only Aramaic. And that's where he made the ultimate sacrifice. But Peter's preaching gave us the earliest gospel, the Gospel of Mark[63]. And his example was enshrined in the Gospel of St. Matthew as the Lord's greatest apostle and the only one who could unify the Jews and the Gentiles, because of his enormous sympathy for both.

As the greatest leader in the early church, Peter gained his reputation by raising up others to positions of leadership in the church and by putting himself into many unfamiliar and dangerous ventures for the sake of Christ. That's the kind of leader we need in our church in renewal. And may the Lord send us many of them!

---

[63] The tradition that Mark was the follower and "interpreter" (i.e., translator from Aramaic to Greek) of St. Peter in his missionary travels was first reported by Eusebius of Caesarea (ca. 260-ca. 339) in his *History of the Church*, Bk II,15; Bk III,39. Says John L. McKenzie, S.J., "Early Christian tradition uniformly attributes the 2nd gospel to Mark, and there is no reason to doubt that this is the John Mark mentioned several times in the NT [New Testament]". *Dictionary of the Bible*, John L. McKenzie, S.J., Bruce, 1965; article: Mark, Gospel of.

The Dream of a Universal (Catholic) Church

The souls of the just are in the hand of God....
In the time of their visitation, they shall shine,
And shall dart about as sparks through stubble. (Wis. 3:1,7)

So far in this book, we have been talking about Catholicism. It is time to look farther forward, time to put on the vision of Jesus or Paul and see what the experience of Catholics will be like when humanity leaves this place of hard national and sectarian bitterness, when it walks out of the dust and darkness of our era and emerges into the sunlight of God's peace. There on the upland lawns of humanity's life here on earth, when we have at last achieved the brother-and-sisterhood with all humanity that we all know is our obligation and our destiny, what will we find? What will our life on earth be like?

If we can catch sight of that vision, we will have some idea of our goal.

Before we begin, it is well to remember the great changes out of which our church developed. Jesus' mission was entirely to the Jews. But the mission of the Jews, whether they were aware of it or not, was to the entire world. Already at the time of Christ, they were dispersed throughout the world. They gave the example of a god-fearing people wherever they lived. The message of the One God had traveled everywhere through their physical presence and their piety. And it was through the Jews that Christianity made its entrance into the world.

We see glimpses of Jesus' ultimate mission to all humanity in the gospels. "Believe me, woman, the hour is coming when you will worship the Father neither on this mountain nor in Jerusalem.... True worshippers will worship the Father in Spirit and Truth.... God is Spirit, and those who worship him must worship in Spirit and truth." (Jn 4:21-24)

But to clear our minds to focus on that future we must first sort out the difference between a church and a religion. So far in this book we have not made that distinction.

Church or Religion?

What was it that Jesus founded? Was it a church or a religion? And what's the difference? In Matthew's gospel, Jesus says, "Thou art Peter and upon this rock I will build my church. And the gates of hell shall not prevail against it."[64] That is probably the strongest institutional statement that Jesus makes in the gospels. And it is easy to misunderstand. The word church here does not mean what we mean by church today. It does not mean a religion. A religion is a system of beliefs and practices by which a certain group of people worship their god or gods. Israel in Jesus' time possessed a religion. Jesus and his companions all belonged to that religion. They practiced it. They believed in its tenets.

So what does it mean when Jesus says, "upon this rock I will build my church"? Clearly, he does not mean to found another religion.

The word used in this passage is the Greek word *ekklesia*. Matthew's is the only gospel to use this word, and he uses it only in this passage and in the parallel passage where he gives the same power of binding and loosing to the laity.[65] The word *ekklesia* means a gathering or group or community. It corresponds to the Hebrew/Aramaic word *qahal*, which was used to signify the assembly of Israel, the crowd of people who followed Moses out of Egypt, for instance. So what Jesus was referring to here was a group of his followers, not a religion. Peter was to have a key role in the formation of this group. And since it does not refer to the founding of a religion, Jesus' statement turns out not to have as strong an institutional meaning as may appear to us so many centuries later.

In fact, Jesus seems to be forming a group that will be a 'leaven' for the whole loaf that is Israel. He wants his followers to be the 'salt of the earth'–people who will be the enlivening ingredient for the religion of Israel. We Catholics now belong to a different religion from Israel, one that has developed its own system of beliefs and practices. If both religions are true, as we believe, the movement or following that Jesus founded is still

---

[64] Mt. 16:18-20
[65] Mt. 18:17-18

called upon to function with respect to religion as a leavening agent.

But if this is true of the religions of Judaism and Christianity, we must ask ourselves if Jesus meant his followers to be the leavening agent for any and every religion, not just Israel or Christianity. Let me explain.

If what Jesus founded was <u>not</u> a religion but rather a group destined to be the exact opposite of a subversive group within Judaism—a group that would bring out Judaism's best aspects—and if Christianity then constructed a religion on top of that movement, what's to prevent our reviving the original movement for the reform of our religion as well, and, for that matter, teaching it to others for the reform of any and all religions?

So what do we mean when we say the Catholic church is something quite different from the Catholic religion? The Catholic religion is the entire organizational structure, the rites, the practices, and almost all of the theology and the sacramentality of Catholicism built up over the centuries since the time of the apostles. The Catholic church, on the other hand, is the great mass of Christ's faithful people who began as a reform movement in Judaism. Out of that very early experience as the apostolic church, they brought the teachings of Jesus Christ, a reverence for the Jewish scriptures, the sacraments of the Eucharist and Baptism, and little else besides a strong morality inherited from the Jews.

Once those early Christians had learned under the guidance of the Holy Spirit to observe the spirit of the Mosaic Law and not the letter, they passed beyond almost all of the habits and customs that make up the Jewish religion, and they had yet to create all of the habits and customs that today make up the Catholic religion. It was this quality that made them seem to some of the Romans to be irreligious. They seemed not to have a religion, and in fact they had very little religion. They were the Christian church without the Christian religion.

Subversion or Subvention?

The approach that the Christian movement of the future must take toward and within the cultures of the world, and within its religions, is the opposite of subversion. We need a new word for this approach. I suggest the word 'subvention.' Subvention means 'a coming to the assistance of.' The action of the Catholic church, that is, of the people who follow Jesus Christ, should be one that comes to the aid of their fellow human beings. It will be one that breaks down barriers between people and lessens the effect that institutions have of keeping people apart.

At the same time, church members will, in effect, be renewing the institutions of which they are members. They will make them more effective, less burdened with meaningless protocols that only hamper them from good actions. 'Good' in this sense means tending toward the fulfillment, the well-being, the respect, and the salvation of human beings. Jesus Christ was the one who said, "Come to me all you who labor and are heavily burdened, and I will refresh you." He was the one who asked us to be revolutionaries, to act from within to improve our religions and our societies, to be leaven for the loaf, salt for the earth, a light for the house, and finally a city seated on a mountain.

As the Book of Wisdom says, "The souls of the just are in the hand of God, and no torment shall touch them.... In the time of their visitation, they shall shine and shall dart about like sparks through stubble." That is, when the Spirit of God calls them to action, they shall not hang back for fear of death. They shall dart about like sparks enkindling the love of God in all their fellow human beings–and it will spread like wildfire. This is perfectly in line with the saying of Jesus, "I have come to set the earth on fire, and how I wish it were already blazing!" (Lk 12:49)

Let us face it, you Catholic people: Jesus Christ was a revolutionary! His movement was not for the lukewarm, for the close-minded, for archconservatives, for defenders of the castle! And it was not for Catholics alone or for Christians–it was for all humanity! The sooner we recognize and adopt that world-view, the sooner we will understand what Jesus came to teach us. According to Jesus Christ, the best way to preserve one's life is to lose it–to spend it regardless of cost–in service to our fellow human beings.

Jesus Christ has shown us how to live. He has given us a movement with few but essential tools to carry us forward. He has told us, in effect, to reform all of our cultural institutions in favor of helping our fellow human beings. Included among these institutions are our religions, our governments, our societies, our workplaces. Nothing in life is to be excluded from kindly concern for our brothers and sisters. No religion, no race, no region, no rule can be exempt from the application of God's love.

Not as in the past will we show the love of God–from the back of a horse or the end of a sword or a gun–but giving our lives in patient labor along with our brothers and sisters, in bearing one another's burdens and supplying one another's needs. God will provide the resources. In the end, all religion, all race, all government will prove immaterial. Only the love of God and our fellow human beings will count. And that will be all sufficient.

Then we will see the barriers between human beings of different religions, races, and political philosophies drop away. Then respect and regard for one another will replace suspicion and distrust. Then we will congratulate one another on the beauty and refinement of each other's culture. We will pride ourselves on appreciating the ingenious insights of each other's religions in leading human beings to God. Then we will recognize that we are all children of the same God, and we will all be able to thank him for sending his Son to show us how to live. And we will celebrate this brother-and-sisterhood with dinners in the Lord's name, with Eucharists.

The End of the Revolution

The end of the revolution will be peace among human beings. Of course, on the way to achieving that end, we will have to develop ways of dealing with aggressors, but those ways will gradually become much different from the ones we use today. They will depend on the solidarity of humankind, on nonaggressive protest, on remonstrances rather than threats, on firm, strong representations to the party who breaks the peace, to the leader who mistreats his native population, to the one who attempts to use weapons against others–that he will certainly and without fail be denied all contact with civilized humanity. No one will deal with him. No one will buy from him or sell to him.

As humanity advances and the community of all humankind becomes a heart-warming, living reality with solidarity its strongest characteristic, ostracism will become a far more serious threat for wrongdoers.

One signpost on the way to peace will be the worldwide recognition that human beings do not have the right to put one another to death–the end of the death penalty. Another will be the disappearance of weapons whose only use is to kill one's fellow human beings.

Our Role

Our role is to pray and to accept responsibility for our life on this earth and for cherishing the lives of all those living with us on this earth. Our role is to be thoughtful, not to be led astray by anyone who comes to us like a wolf in sheep's clothing, whether it be the television set that distracts us from thinking seriously about our life, or overabsorption in sports or work or popular spectacles or any other drugs, or even in the demands made on us by religious "authorities." Test everything, as St. Paul says, and obey your conscience. You are responsible for your life. No one else is. "I was only obeying orders" will not work as an excuse at the Last Judgment.

Even St. Paul was surprised to find his life turned completely around from the assumptions and convictions he had previously held. It was God who recognized the sincerity of his life and credited him for it. Paul was wrong to wish to put people to death because they believed differently from him. But all his life he had made a sincere effort to know where his obligation lay. If we make the same kind of sincere effort, God will not let us go astray.

As for the details, we have the Holy Spirit and each other. God will supply whatever we lack. It is up to you to create the universal (catholic) church of the future, the entire Assembly of All Humankind Under God. You have the tools. Let's see what you can do with them!

The Beginning...

Bibliography

Some of the works listed here were instrumental in bringing me to the conclusions I have reached in this book. Others are simply the best sources I know of that will give the student (i.e., disciple) a well rounded view of the life of Jesus Christ and the history of the Catholic church. Others–the theological titles–are given here with the warning that they present the church's doctrine as the hierarchy permits it to be taught. They are worth reading with the caveat that anything they say that touches on governance must be considered self-interested and highly suspect. I have tried and, I hope, succeeded in keeping this list of books to a minimum. Unfortunately, some of these titles are now out of print.

Sources

The New American Bible, eds. Louis F. Hartman, C.SS.R., P.W. Skehan, Stephen J. Hartdegen, O.F.M., et al.; Cath. Bible Press, Nashville, 1,488 p., 1986

Translated from the original texts. Especially good introductions and notes. Draws on the latest scholarship.

The Jerusalem Bible, ed. Alexander Jones et al., Doubleday, NY, 2,056 p., 1966

Translated from the original texts with attention paid to the translations made for *La "Bible de Jerusalem."* This French Bible set the standard for Catholic Bibles when it appeared in 1956, both for the vivid accuracy of its translations and for the up-to-date scholarship of its notes. The English version of this Bible features the same notes translated from French with slight updating.

Des sacrements, des mystères; ed., tr. & annot. by Dom Bernard Botte, O.S.B., Éditions du Cerf; Paris; 1949

Ambrose, the author of these two works on the sacraments and the mysteries of Christianity, was the last Western Church father to read and write Greek. He was also a friend and correspondent of the Eastern Church father, St. Basil. Elected bishop of Milan at age

131

35 before he had even been baptized, he was compelled, in his own words, "to teach what he had not learned." He was a quick study, however, and eloquent. In his writings, we get a snapshot of what Catholic Christians understood the meaning of their religion and their church to be in the West in the fourth century. In his sermons on the sacraments, *De Sacramentis*, he provides a text of the Canon of the Mass in Milan at that time and his explanation of its significance.

The Apostolic Tradition, St. Hippolytus of Rome, ed. by Gregory Dix, S.P.C.K., London, lxxxii, 90 p., 1937, 1968
Reveals the mind-set of a hierarchy-in-the-making nearly a century before Constantine freed Catholics from oppression, when there were no church buildings and no altars and when bishops were elected by their fellow Christians as a matter of course.

The Apostolic Fathers, Kirsopp Lake tr., Harvard Univ. Press, Cambridge, MA, Wm Heinemann, London, vol 1, 409 p., vol 2, 396 p., 1912, with many reprints
From the Loeb Classical Library, these two, small volumes contain nine pieces of early Christian literature, including *1 Clement*, the letters of Ignatius of Antioch, and the *Didache* or "Teaching of the Twelve Apostles," with Greek text and facing English translation. The translations have some imperfections.

Ante-Nicene Christian Library: Translations of the Writings of the Fathers down to CE 325. Vol. II: Justin Martyr and Athenagoras, ed. by A. Roberts and J. Donaldson, T. & T. Clark, Edinburgh, 465 p., 1867
Justin Martyr was a pagan, born in Samaria ca. 110 CE. A teacher of philosophy, he was converted to Christianity and was the first to use Greek philosophy to explain Christianity, thereby inventing theology. Three complete works survive. In his *First Apology*, addressed to the emperor, Antoninus Pius, he describes the Christian mysteries of Baptism and the Eucharist as practiced ca. 153-155 CE. He was martyred in 165 CE.

L'Ordinaire de la Messe: Texte Critique, Traduction et Études, Bernard Botte, O.S.B. et Christine Mohrmann, Cerf, Paris, 152 p., 1953

A critical text of the Roman Mass as established by the Council of Trent with French translation and studies of individual words by two accomplished scholars of early Christian literature.

Prex Eucharistica: Textus e Variis Liturgiis Antiquioribus Selecti, ed. Anton Hänggi, Irmgard Pahl, Universitätsverlag Freiburg Schweiz, 517 p., 1968, 1998

A comprehensive collection of early Eucharistic prayers, or anaphoras, and related documents gathered by a team of liturgical scholars. It includes New Testament texts, translations into Latin of the earliest available Jewish liturgical texts, and examples of early Mass prayers from many different Eastern and Western traditions, with Greek text where available and Latin translations throughout.

La Struttura Letteraria della Preghiera Eucharistica, Cesare Giraudo, Pontificio Istituto Biblico, Roma, 388 p., 1989

Giraudo, who received his doctorate in theology from the Gregorian University in Rome, sheds light on the antecedents of the Eucharistic prayer in the Old Testament and in Jewish liturgy. He analyzes a number of early anaphoras (Eucharistic prayers) to show how they exhibit the ancient literary form.

Reference

Dictionary of the Bible, John L. McKenzie, S.J., Bruce, Milwaukee, 954 p., 1965

A one-volume encyclopedia of the Bible by one of the foremost Catholic scriptural scholars of the 20th century. A brilliant, well-balanced work.

The New Jerome Biblical Commentary, eds. Raymond E. Brown, S.S., Joseph A. Fitzmyer, S.J., Roland E. Murphy, O.Carm., Prentice Hall, Englewood Cliffs, NJ, 1,475 p., 1990

This is a total reworking of the path-breaking Jerome Biblical Commentary that appeared in 1968. Two-thirds of the material is

new. The editors are among the greatest biblical scholars in the
world. They each edited part of the work of 74 contributors. A very
solid and reliable commentary.

Handbook for Biblical Studies, Nicholas Turner, Westminster
Press, Phila, PA, 144 p., 1982
    Technical terms are the bane of the novice scripture student.
Nevertheless, the study of scripture can be a minefield without
them and the insights they embody. This brief handbook is highly
enlightening.

Dictionary of Theology, Karl Rahner, Herbert Vorgrimler, tr. by
Richard Strachan, David Smith, Robert Nowell, and Sarah O'Brien
Twohig, Crossroad, NY, 541 p., 1981
    Half of the articles in this volume were contributed by Karl
Rahner, the foremost Catholic theologian of the 20th century; the
other half by Herbert Vorgrimler, himself a solid and balanced
theologian. A useful synopsis of Catholic theology since Vatican
II, always with the warning, Don't trust what they say about
church governance.

Christian Origins

*Antioch and Rome: New Testament Cradles of Catholic
Christianity*, Raymond E. Brown, S.S., and John P. Meier, Paulist
Press, NY, 242 p., 1983
    Two of the greatest New Testament scholars of the 20th century
combined to write this study of two of the first centers of Jewish-
gentile Christianity. Meier, a specialist in Matthew, studied three
generations of Christianity at Antioch. Brown studied three
generations at Rome. Together they produced unforgettable results.

*The Vision of Matthew: Christ, Church, and Morality in the First
Gospel*, John P. Meier, Crossroad, NY, 270 p., 1991
    Matthew's gospel is Meier's specialty. In this book he gives us
a close reading of the gospel that has been called 'the gospel of the
church.' According to Father Ray Brown, "Meier is clearly first in
American Catholic scholars on Matthew."

The Churches the Apostles Left Behind, Raymond E. Brown, Paulist Press, NY, 156 p., 1984

Raymond E. Brown, S.S., analyzes seven churches in the subapostolic period that managed to continue after the death of the apostles. To discover how they survived, he studies the New Testament writings that were addressed to them by Paul, Peter, John, and Matthew.

The Beginnings of the Church, Frederick J. Cwiekowski, S.S., Paulist Press, NY, 222 p., 1988

With a foreword and endorsement by Father Ray Brown, S.S., one of the greatest New Testament scholars of the 20th century, as showing "an informed awareness of the complexity of church developments since the first century," acquaintance with "a broad span of New Testament research," and "a centrist approach, relying on what one can reasonably substantiate in the biblical data," this book is a 'must read' for anyone who wants to know how the Catholic church came to be.

Women and Ministry in the New Testament, Elisabeth M. Tetlow, Paulist Press, NY, 164 p., 1980

Compares favorably with *The Beginnings of the Church* by Cwiekowski, but explores more fully the role of women in founding the Catholic church.

On Consulting the Faithful in Matters of Doctrine, John Henry Newman, ed. John Coulson, Sheed & Ward, NY, 118 p., 1961

This wonderful essay, first published in 1859, shows how for 60 years during the 4th century the laity preserved the true Catholic faith when every bishop and the pope either professed Arianism or was forced by the emperor to subscribe to it–a clear instance of the failure of the hierarchy's supposed *magisterium*. Newman's career in the church suffered greatly because of this essay.

Church History

Saints & Sinners: A History of the Popes, Eamon Duffy, Yale Univ. Press, New Haven, 462 p., 1997, 2001

A vivid, highly acclaimed, and absorbing work of scholarship that spans the nearly 20 centuries of Catholic church history from the time of Sts. Peter and Paul to the papacy of John Paul II. The author is a Catholic and president of Magdalene College, Cambridge.

The Oxford Dictionary of Popes, J.D.N. Kelly, Oxford Univ. Press, Oxford, 347 p., 1986

Scholarly and balanced lives of all the popes and antipopes in their historical and religious setting by a distinguished church historian and Anglican priest.

The Catholic Church: A Short History, Hans Küng, tr. by John Bowden, Modern Library, NY, 221 p., 2001

A remarkable account of the founding and development of the Christian religion, which sets in perspective the situation of the Catholic church today.

New Testament

An Introduction to the New Testament, Raymond E. Brown, S.S., 1 vol., Doubleday Anchor Bible Reference Library, NY, 878 p., 1997

This book is written for the student of the New Testament. It focuses solely on the texts of the New Testament and not on the early church, which would have been a much larger topic. It does provide introductions to scriptural study and to the religious, philosophical, political, and social world of the New Testament, as well as summaries of each book, an appendix on the historical Jesus and discussions of important theological points. An excellent handbook.

The Death of the Messiah: From Gethsemane to the Grave, Raymond E. Brown, S.S., 2 vols., Doubleday Anchor Bible Reference Library, NY, 1,608 p., 1994

This is one of the best examples of how scholars go about studying the scriptures. Brown takes the longest connected accounts of the life of Jesus, the passion narratives, and studies them in great detail to determine what we can know about the death of

Jesus historically. The narratives sometimes contradict one another, but Brown supplies all of the data and arguments necessary for the reader to make up his or her own mind.

New Testament Theology, Joachim Jeremias, tr. by John Bowden, Chas Scribner's Sons, NY, 330 p., 1971
A profound work that summarizes the best that German scholarship had to offer up to the time of its publication. Jeremias had a thorough grasp of the scholarship, the scriptures, and the Jewish background of Jesus.

The Quest for the Historical Jesus

A Marginal Jew: Rethinking the Historical Jesus, John P. Meier, 3 vols., Doubleday Anchor Bible Reference Library, 2,305 p., 1991, 1994, 2001
A thorough and well balanced reconsideration of all of the 20th century scholarly literature bearing on the Quest for the Historical Jesus. Meier carries out on a much more massive scale the work begun by Albert Schweitzer in his comprehensive analysis of 19th century scholarship on the historical Jesus. Meier surveys and analyzes a worldwide literature two or three times as extensive as Schweitzer's. The as yet unpublished fourth volume of his study promises to provide the clearest possible portrait of the historical Jesus ever achieved.

Jesus and Judaism, E.P. Sanders, Fortress Press, Phila, PA, 444 p., 1985
John P. Meier said that this book "embodies a generation's desire to avoid exaggerations from right or left...and (tries) to understand what [Jesus] meant to say and accomplish." The book can have no higher praise. It is one of several excellent books by Sanders.

Jesus Within Judaism, ed. by James H. Charlesworth, Doubleday Anchor Bible Reference Library, NY, 265 p., 1988
Remarkable insights into Jesus and his time supplied by recent archeology conveyed by this renowned scholar of Old Testament

pseudepigrapha (anonymous intertestamental literature). One of many excellent books from the Anchor Bible Reference Library.

Jerusalem in the Time of Jesus, Joachim Jeremias, tr. by F.H. & C.H. Cave and M.E. Dahl, Fortress Press, Phila., 405 p., 1969
The best one-volume summary of the social-cultural-religious fabric of the city of Jerusalem during Jesus' lifetime.

Jesus the Jew, Geza Vermes, Macmillan, NY, 286 p., 1973
An interesting view of Jesus in his own time and of the titles that were ascribed to him written by a scholar of Judaica and Fellow of Oxford University.

The Sacraments

Sacramental Theology, Herbert Vorgrimler, tr. Linda M. Maloney, Liturgical Press, Collegeville, MN, 329 p., 1987, 1992
This is as good a summary of Catholic teaching on the sacraments as can be found. It deals well with their emergence, their history, and their theology since Vatican II.

Today's Situation

Papal Sin: Structures of Deceit, Garry Wills, Doubleday, NY, 326 p., 2000
Gives many examples to show that the pope and the hierarchy rely on lies to support their power structure and that this has fostered a culture of deceit throughout the hierarchy of the Catholic church.

Cardinal Ratzinger: The Vatican's Enforcer of the Faith, John L. Allen, Jr., Continuum, NY, 340 p., 2000
Traces the career of one who was a *peritus* (expert theologian) and a liberal force against the conservative Curia at Vatican II through various stages to the point where he became the highly conservative head of the Congregation for the Doctrine of the Faith, the destroyer of liberation theology in the 1980s and 1990s, and the true successor of the Grand Inquisitor, now Pope Benedict

XVI. By the Vatican affairs reporter for the (U.S.) *National Catholic Reporter.*

The Silencing of Leonardo Boff: The Vatican and the Future of World Christianity, Harvey Cox, Meyer-Stone, Oak Park, IL, 208 p., 1988

Examines, with balance and deep understanding of the Catholic church, the treatment by the Vatican of a Franciscan priest and one of the leading proponents of liberation theology during the 1980s. The author is a Protestant and was then professor of divinity at Harvard Divinity School, Cambridge, MA.

Governance in the Spirit

Sharing Wisdom: A Process for Group Decision Making, Mary Benet McKinney, O.S.B., Tabor, Allen, TX, 168 p., 1987

Sr. Mary Benet in this book proposes a method of decision making for Catholic groups and organizations that can't possibly work, and yet it does. Voting, she says, makes winners and losers; consensus decision making takes into account everyone's opinion and calls for a unanimous decision. She taps the church's deepest roots to discover a method to employ discernment of spirits. In the process, often the opinion of the most neglected minority wins everyone's support. If your group can survive the first use of this method, you will find it indispensable. But be sure and train the newcomers. This method of decision making is preferable to both monarchical fiat and democratic voting.

Timeline of Key Works and Passages
Dealing with Christian Origins
In the First, Second, and Third Centuries

Time in Church's Life	Work, Author, Date Composed	Significance	Discovery of the Text/General Availability for Study
30-35 CE (80-90 CE)	Acts 2:42-46, St. Luke, 80-90 CE	The ordinary followers of Jesus are celebrating the Eucharist in their homes ("the breaking of the bread"). This passage looks back to the situation shortly after Jesus' death in the 30s. Obviously at the time of Luke's writing the situation has not changed essentially or he would have indicated that fact somewhere in Acts.	Sometime after the turn of the first century (100 CE)
ca. 56 CE	1 Cor. 11:17-29, St. Paul, ca. 56 CE	St. Paul upbraids the Corinthians for what was reported to him as occurring in a house church. Some were eating and drinking (to excess) as if the Eucharist were an ordinary meal. They had no conception of what we today call 'the real presence' of Jesus within the 'elements' of bread and wine. Paul complains of their failure to recognize the Lord Jesus in the bread and the wine. He does not complain of their lack of ordination in celebrating the Eucharist.	This is one of Paul's earliest letters. It would have been known in Corinth ca. 56 CE. It would have spread to the rest of the church in succeeding decades as word of its existence spread and people managed to make copies.

Time in Church's Life	Work, Author, Date Composed	Significance	Discovery of the Text/General Availability for Study
ca. 96 CE	1 Clement to the Corinthians, Anon., 75-110 CE	Written by the Secretary of the Roman congregations to the church at Corinth to convince them to accept back the leaders [bishops or overseers and presbyters or elders] they have deposed. Praises a leadership structure for the church similar to that of the Roman army (Ch 37). Says that Peter and Paul were put to death on account of "unrighteous zeal," probably the envy of existing Roman church leaders. No bishop [overseer] in Rome at this time, otherwise Clement would bear that title. Says that leaders are appointed "with the consent of the whole church" (44:3).	At one time this letter was considered to be part of the New Testament. Manuscripts exist in Greek (the language of the Roman church for the first 250 years of its existence; the language in which Clement was written), and Syriac, Latin, and Coptic translations.
90-110 CE	The *Didache*, the Teaching of the Twelve Apostles, Anon., 90-110 CE	Contains the earliest known Eucharistic prayer (Did. X:2-5). Also describes the Christian community at the point where it is transitioning from a leadership consisting of prophets and teachers, the model described in Acts and in the authentic letters of Paul, to a leadership elected by the community, consisting of 'overseers' (bishops) and deacons (Did XV:1-2). The overseers are not yet monarchical bishops.	Unknown to scholars and church historians until 1875 when it was discovered in the Patriarchal Library of Jerusalem at Constantinople. After its publication, it required decades to analyze its contents and establish its significance.

Time in Church's Life	Work, Author, Date Composed	Significance	Discovery of the Text/General Availability for Study
ca. 107 CE	Seven Letters to the Churches, Ignatius of Antioch, ca. 107 CE	Ignatius is being taken by Roman soldiers from Antioch in Syria to Rome where he will be put to death for the faith. En route, he writes letters to the Christian churches along the way to encourage them in the faith *but also to advance the notion of the monarchical bishop as the leader of each individual church.* In each case, he writes to the bishop, if that church has a bishop. Even so, his letters testify to the fact that (1) he himself as bishop shares authority equally with the group of elders and the group of deacons in his church, (2) not every church has a bishop–and chiefly Rome at this date does not have a bishop, since the Roman church has evidently continued the Jewish practice of election of synagogue (church) elders as leaders.	Sometime after 107 CE. Ignatius's letters have been available in the church since the second century. They were translated into Syriac, Sahidic, Armenian, and Latin. Like many other Christian documents–most famously St. Paul–they have been subject to anonymous imitation. This resulted in a *long recension* of 13 letters and a *short recension* of seven letters. Scholarship has largely recovered the original seven letters.

Time in Church's Life	Work, Author, Date Composed	Significance	Discovery of the Text/General Availability for Study
153-155 CE	Justin Martyr's *Apologies*	Provides an account of Christian church life and teaching during the middle of the second century. There is no discernible hierarchy, possibly because Justin does not want to identify church leaders in an age of persecutions. The only church officer mentioned is the deacon. We know from the *Didache* 50 years earlier and from Hippolytus's *Apostolic Tradition* 60 years later that in Justin's time church leaders were elected by the people. Mass prayers were said extemporaneously by the celebrant "to the best of his abilities" [LXVI, 5].	This work has come down to us, miraculously, in a single manuscript preserved in the National Library in Paris, France, a manuscript copied in 1364. It began to receive the close attention of many scholars only in the latter half of the 19th century.

Time in Church's Life	Work, Author, Date Composed	Significance	Discovery of the Text/General Availability for Study
ca. 215 CE	Hippolytus's *Apostolic Tradition*	This work describes the Eucharist and the ordination of a bishop, as well as Baptism, Confirmation, and the ordinations of a presbyter and a deacon, at the beginning of the 3rd century, while the Christian church was still subject to persecution. It vividly shows the movement toward a model of priesthood similar to that portrayed in the Jewish scriptures–in the minds of those exercising leadership in the church at that time–despite their inability in a time of persecution to establish Temples and altars similar to those described in the Jewish scriptures. As conservative a picture of growing clericalism as it paints, however, Hippolytus's work portrays the bishop as elected by the people as late as the third century.	One of the most remarkable examples of scholarly detective work on record. A 1916 monograph by Dom R.H. Connolly got the search started by suggesting that a number of 4th, 5th and 6th century church documents in Ethiopic, Coptic, Syriac, Arabic, and Latin all must have this early 3rd century Greek church order as their source. That began a work of scholarly comparison and translation and a search for fragments of the original Greek which resulted in the recovery of the lost *Apostolic Tradition* of Hippolytus. The *AT* was first published in English in 1934, followed by the first critical edition in English by Dom Gregory Dix in 1937 of a work that had been lost for more than 1700 years.

Index

About the Author

Joseph Marren is a Chicago Catholic and a late bloomer as an author. He has an A.B. from Loyola University Chicago (1957; major in Latin, minor in history) and an M.A. from the University of Kentucky (1958; major in ancient languages–Latin and Ancient Greek–minor in linguistics). He has a nodding acquaintance with several European languages and has been a student of Church history for more that 50 years.

His working life has been divided among editing, public relations, and sales and administrative support. For his first job out of college, he edited a four-volume Catholic missal, one of whose contributors was the then-unknown Father Andrew Greeley, who wrote introductions to the four volumes. Greeley needed a lot of editing, Joe recalls.

Otherwise, his life has been unexceptional. He did spend a year in Panama as a boy on the eve of WWII. His father worked in the Canal Zone and Joe was sent to what turned out to be an all Spanish-speaking Catholic school for first grade; he knew no Spanish, and his father, a widower, was unaware of the language situation. Joe finally learned to read English in Panamanian summer school. Shortly after Pearl Harbor he and his younger brother flew back to the U.S. on a DC-3 airliner, a life-long memory.

Joe is married to Mary Hereley Marren, whom he met when she was the first woman editor-in-chief of the Loyola University *News* and he a reporter. They raised nine children, all now college graduates and married. Besides their children, they dote on their 17 grandchildren.

Joe wrote the first chapter of this book in 1998 to explain to his family why he remained a Catholic. The rest of the book, calling for a revival of lay leadership of the Catholic church and an unseating of the current clerical leaders, was written in reaction to the predator-priest scandal that made news in Boston in 2002.

Since writing *Talking Treason*, Joe believes that all bishops should be recalled and recertified by consensus-decision-making elections in their own dioceses and that they should run against opposing candidates from the laity, both women and men.

Breinigsville, PA USA
26 November 2010
250003BV00004B/293/P